Facing the Wrath

Confronting the Right in Dangerous Times

Sara Diamond

Common Courage Press   Monroe, Maine

Library of Congress Cataloging-in-Publication Data
Diamond, Sara
Facing the wrath : confronting the right in dangerous
times / Sara Diamond.
      p.   cm.
Includes index.
ISBN 1-56751-079-5. (cloth)
-- ISBN 1-56751-078-7
1.(paper)
Conservatism--United States. 2. United States--Politics
and government--1945-1989. 3. United States--Politics
and government--1989-   I.Title.
JC573.2.U6D525   1996
320.5'2'0973--dc20   95-47021
                  CIP

Common Courage Press
P.O. Box 702
Monroe ME 04951
207-525-0900
Fax: 207-525-3068

First Printing

For Richard

Contents

Part III
The Patriot Movement

Introduction

Why Study the Right

Among its many effects, the Oklahoma City bombing drove public interest in right-wing movements to an all-time high. Timothy McVeigh was the first suspect arrested, and before the ink was dry on his arrest warrant, reporters started trying to put their spin on the story.

I spoke with a reporter from the Associated Press who was trying to figure out where paramilitary violence came from. She was responsible for putting the rise of right-wing militia groups into context for readers nationwide. Yet she had no knowledge of the recent history of paramilitary organizations in the United States. She was incredulous when I told her that in the mid-1980s, white supremacist groups had waged a short reign of terror in the northwest and the Rockies, including the assassination of a Denver radio talk show host. After I told her of a series of armed robberies conducted by members of the Aryan Nations, her editor insisted that she call me back to demand proof. I suggested that they ought to look in the AP data base to retrieve their own wire service reports of just a decade ago.

A network television producer called, eager to frame the Oklahoma City bombing in the context of a "history of political violence." She wanted to know what I thought of the idea, and I suggested that she could examine the recent history of paramilitary groups and also the wave of abortion clinic bombings over the past decade. But that was not what she had in mind. She wanted to link the arrest of Timothy McVeigh to the leftist Weather Underground of the 1970s. Her thesis was that political violence from the Left was as rampant as that coming from the Right, and that all terrorists were driven by the same psychological disturbances. I suggested that if she was intent on looking at psychological rather than political motives for murder and mayhem, perhaps she could do a psychological profile of former

President George Bush. She didn't get it. I had to explain that Bush had presided over the killing of tens of thousands of people in Iraq just a few years ago. I added that she might include a look at former Marine Lt. Col. Oliver North, who had aided in the killing of civilians in Central America in the 1980s. She said: "yeah, he's probably crazy."

We can blame the mainstream media for its poor handling of events and trends involving right-wing groups and individuals deemed beyond the pale. Or we can view these two reporters as broadly representative of the kind of ill-informed, shortsighted thinking applied to countless topics in the news, including the nature and implications of right-wing movement activity. These two professionals in the media industry are not much different than many other people trying to figure out what the Right is all about.

***

It was New Year's Day, 1995, two days after an apparently deranged young man named John Salvi allegedly shot up two Boston area abortion clinics and killed two women who worked there. I got a phone message from a veteran pro-choice and pro-gressive movement activist. His group wanted some ideas for planning demonstrations, and he wanted to ask me about "connections" between the anti-abortion movement, corporations and hate groups.

It was an honest question but one with no simple answers. It was a question framed by some persistent assumptions about the nature of the U.S. right wing. It is true that some anti-abortion groups have received corporate donations, and there have been some cases of overlap between anti-abortion and white suprema-cist groups. But by looking for whatever evidence might cast the "pro-lifers" superficially in the worst possible light, my acquain-tance, I thought, missed the point. In the days following the shootings in Massachusetts, most anti-abortion organizations condemned John Salvi's vile deed. But others in the movement came out of the woodwork to publicly advocate "justifiable homicide" against abortion clinic workers.

Mostly anti-abortion groups have been funded through small

donations from members. Most have steered clear of linking abortion to themes of racial bigotry. Mostly the anti-abortion movement has spent two decades issuing propaganda about "baby killers," "abortuaries" and "holocausts." That constant drumbeat, and the relentless grassroots activism of thousands of people, inevitably led to rising frustrations and a drive toward vigilante violence by a minority of the movement. During twelve years of symbiotic ties between the Christian Right and the Reagan-Bush administrations, the federal government had been loathe to adequately investigate—let alone prosecute— more than a handful of those responsible for clinic violence. Why look for ties to marginal hate groups when the real strength underlying the anti-abortion movement has been its political influence within the Republican Party? Why zero in on corporate donations—as much if not more of such money goes to pro-choice groups—when the anti-abortion movement has relied largely on volunteer labor and a support base of thousands of activists?

To challenge the entrenched clout of right-wing movements and organizations, critics must know how the opposition really operates. For progressive people, I am convinced, that means abandoning some pre-conceived stereotypes about right-wing adversaries. It means knowing the gory details, like connections to hate groups. But it also means coming to terms with the Right's popular, grassroots base of support. It means seeing right-wing movements not as mere puppets for big business. It means looking beyond the psychotics who make headlines with their bloody deeds to see that most activists on the Right work quietly and diligently, using accepted tactics of political influence. It means facing the wrath that comes not just from big, anonymous government agencies and corporate power, but also from some of our own fellow citizens—ordinary people working overtime to effect a thoroughly reactionary policy agenda.

We cannot understand even shocking, criminal actions unless we examine the milieu that fosters the Timothy McVeighs and John Salvis of our society. We need to become familiar with the names, faces, methods of operation and, perhaps most importantly, the underlying philosophies of right-wing movements. Progressives avoid such knowledge at the risk of making unwise choices about what to do and with whom to ally.

Here is a case in point. During the Persian Gulf war and its aftermath, a number of progressives fell hook-line-and-sinker for the rhetorical pitches of demagogues and conspiracy theorists from the far right end of the political spectrum. Pacifica radio stations, long known as reliable sources of alternative public affairs broadcasts, promoted Bo Gritz, Craig Hulet and other luminaries of the far Right as if they were reputable analysts for the Left. Out of ignorance, Pacifica programmers misread the far Right's opposition to the Gulf War as a green light for a putative alliance. Those who fell to overtures from right-wing conspiracy theorists could not—or, in a few cases, would not—hear that anti-government rhetoric in itself did not imply laudable policy goals. For many years, clever operatives from the far Right made efforts to promote themselves as sources of information and analysis for the Left.

At the same time, it was not until the 1990s that the Left began to take seriously the political threat posed by the massive Christian Right. Because the movement's millions of foot soldiers were misunderstood as just a bunch of religious zealots, the Left forfeited its chance to counter-organize while the Christian Right rose to prominence in the 1980s, largely by working hand-in-glove with Republican policymakers.

Ineffectiveness in confronting the growth of right-wing movements has been due largely, in my view, to the Left's failure to see the full scope of our opposition. (By "the Left," I refer neither to liberal lobbying groups nor to the elitist clique that calls itself the Democratic Party. I refer to the small but grassroots movements for true egalitarianism in all spheres of life.) Elected officials and agencies of the state, by and large, represent and respond to corporate power. We on the Left have a hard enough time trying to figure out how to break the corporate stranglehold on what might otherwise be democratic forms of policymaking. But what sustains the prevailing system goes beyond the most powerful and visible agents of the state and the almighty dollar. Countless thousands of our own fellow citizens, organized effectively into right-wing social movements over many decades, play a key role in sustaining the existing political-economic system and all its attendant outrages. The Left will never win the kind of policies that would ensure the basic needs and rights of all without taking on the myriad forces working to maintain inequality—along class, race, and gender lines. The corporate class and the political elites who feed at its trough could not do their dirty work, in a procedural democracy, without the active and passive consent of the governed. Right-wing movements, often at odds with this or that particular policy or piece of legislation, nevertheless are what I call "system-supportive" of the status quo. They are part of the glue that holds the whole system together, and they do so in some consistent and predictable ways.

Critics of the Right are often confused by the nature of the Right's seemingly contradictory stance toward the uses of government power. People on the Right, for example, tend to favor the death penalty but oppose legal abortion. (Here the distinction revolves around the line between criminal guilt versus innocent "pre-born" life.) They tend to favor tough law enforcement but they also want the government to look the other way when businesses make profit while endangering or defrauding the public.

The Right's seemingly selective pro- and anti-government positions are a conundrum for the Left—until one sees that there are consistent patterns in the Right's orientation toward the state. We can see the patterns if we think about the Right's activities and positions historically and generally—there are exceptions to every rule. In the post-World War II era, the Right backed a deadly nuclear arms race and U.S. military intervention all over the world. The Right also backed government repression of dissident groups at home, from the McCarthy and civil rights eras, through the disruption of peace groups in the 1980s.

In the realm of social policy, the Right wants the government to outlaw abortion, and restrict access to contraception and pornography. They oppose gender pay equity, and they have opposed federal funding of childcare, which would ease the burden of working mothers. They support initiatives that would permanently condemn gays and lesbians to second-class citizenship. In essence, the Right wants the government to enforce behavioral conformity to Biblical morality and to maintain traditionally unequal relationships between men and women.

At the same time, the Right invokes an apparently anti-government stance when it comes to regulating businesses: on environmental standards, workplace and product safety, adherence to labor laws. In the 1990s, the Right stakes its claim on opposing the affirmative action policies that, however flawed in practice, were designed to better distribute career opportunities to subordinate groups.

The same right-wing groups that want big government to police disorder and immorality cry foul against those parts of the government involved in protecting the many from the few. To be characteristically "right-wing," then, is to endorse some government functions and policies and to oppose others. In other words, the Right holds a coherent and consistent set of positions regarding the proper role of the *state*. Some theorists view the state as merely the organizational embodiment of a society's wealthiest members, hence the term "ruling class." I draw my view of the state from the work of the renowned Italian Marxist Antonio Gramsci, who theorized the state as the entire set of agencies, officeholders and even extra-governmental institutions responsible for preserving the structure of power and wealth in a society. The state involves coercive bureaucracies such as police and military agencies. But it also involves consent-winning institutions, such as schools, churches and the mass media. The latter set of players are not necessarily tied directly to the top economic class, though they typically act on its behalf.

In any event, we can see from the pattern of movement activities and philosophical positions that the Right favors a strong role for the state when it comes to *enforcing* order at home or abroad, be that through the means of the military, police or religiously inspired codes of conduct. At the same time, the Right wants the state to refrain from *distributing* wealth, power and legal rights more equitably throughout society. In the policy realm, the Right opposes the government when it taxes the rich, provides for the poor, regulates business, or intervenes against racially or gender-based discrimination.

What appears to be a contradictory stance toward the role of state power is, in fact, a quite consistent one. The Right has consistently rallied around three general tendencies: support for militarism (including domestic police power), traditional morality, and laissez-faire capitalist economics. In my book *Roads to*

Dominion, I document and analyze the centrality of militarism, traditional moralism and support for unrestrained capitalism in a fifty-year history of right-wing movements in the United States.

There are exceptions from time to time and they, too, underscore the broader patterns. In the 1990s, some on the Right opposed the United States' entry into multilateral economic treaties such as NAFTA and GATT. Presidential candidates Patrick Buchanan and Ross Perot, in 1992, drew support for their opposition to these treaties. But right-wing opposition to NAFTA and GATT, unlike the stance of the Left, had nothing to do with wanting to prevent big business from tightening its grip on labor at home and south of the border. The rightists who opposed NAFTA and GATT invoked the traditionally *nationalist* current in right-wing thinking. They worried that the United States would lose its "sovereignty," i.e., its ability to dictate to other countries by forming the kind of "entangling alliances" George Washington cautioned against.

Nationalism also drove a minority on the Right to oppose the Persian Gulf war—not because lives were at stake but because Desert Storm set a precedent for United Nations-led military interventions. The trouble with the United Nations is that it cannot be relied upon to act one hundred percent in the interests of U.S. elites.

Similarly, the Right's reaction to abuses by domestic law enforcement agencies has been selective and hypocritical. Since President George Bush declared his War on Drugs, countless people have had their homes broken into and property seized illegally because police agents said they were looking for drugs. The prisons are filled with young people, especially African American men, serving long sentences for mere possession of illegal drugs. Yet few on the Right have a problem with this form of law enforcement, let alone with routine police violence, a la the Rodney King incident. Only following a pair of law enforcement fiascos—the fatal 1992 shooting of the wife and son of Idaho white supremacist Randy Weaver and the massacre of eighty-plus Branch Davidians in 1993—has the Right become preoccupied with police abuses. The Second Amendment rightfully protects gun ownership but it does not authorize weapons enthusiasts to resist any and all arrest warrants. Nor does right-wing demagoguery over Waco and violence in the movies address the roots of the violent crime we all fear.

The essays included in this book do not theorize the relationships between right-wing movements and state institutions in abstract terms. Nor is the Right's set of policy preferences solely an academic question, as some of the above discussion might imply. In the 1990s, as in earlier decades, the Right has made itself central to political controversies that take their toll in human suffering. The damage has been incalculable.

This collection of essays covers some of the right-wing organizations that were involved in aiding and abetting U.S. sponsored wars in the 1980s and 1990s. In these years, some of the United States' foreign affairs operations have been conducted under the euphemistic rubric of "low intensity warfare" in Central America and elsewhere. By providing so-called humanitarian aid to proxy armies, and through relentless propaganda campaigns at home, the Christian Right, along with secular rightwing think tanks and lobbies, bolstered the goals of the White House, against the better judgment of most of the U.S. public. Leaders such as Pat Robertson, organizations such as the Heritage Foundation and the Free Congress Foundation, bear much of the blame for the tens of thousands of civilians who were killed in the name of anticommunism in recent years. Similarly, the policy analysts ensconced in right-wing think tanks such as the Rand Corporation helped anesthetize the U.S. public from the horrors of what the U.S. government did in the Persian Gulf in 1991. The Right was not unified over the prosecution of the Gulf War. Patrick Buchanan and other prominent rightists who had spent years promoting U.S. militarism were reluctant to commit U.S. armed forces to a post-Communist conflict. But their voices were drowned out by the majority on the Right who, after decades of anticommunist organizing, were not about to lay down the sword. The end result of majority right-wing support for the Bush administration was the annihilation of tens of thousands of human beings and the further destabilization of the entire Middle East region.

In most cases, the influence of the Right can be considered in light of what has not happened, as much as in terms of what has. What if the Right had not opposed public funding for AIDS education, and had not continuously stigmatized homosexual people? How many lives might have been saved? What if anti-abortion vigilantes had not terrorized clinics, and feminist activists had not had to spend most of their resources in defense of reproductive choice? Absent the continuous threat to earlier gains, a women's movement might have forged ahead on policies for pay equity and federally funded childcare and health care.

On race matters, the organized Right has kept the civil rights movement stalled at the point of defending the gains of the 1960s. What if civil rights activists had been free to pursue more equitable representation for voters of color in the 1990s? What might have been some of the ripple effects of economic progress for people of color—in lowering rates of teen delinquency, in easing hostile attitudes toward new immigrants, in countless other aspects of life for millions of people?

We can only imagine where our society would be headed now absent the power of right-wing movements, working in sync with corrupt and entrenched political elites. Nor should we think of the impact of the Right exclusively in terms of elections. The Right wages its so-called "culture war" not just through formal legislative processes but also through its very own cultural institutions. Readers will notice my frequent attention to the Christian Right's religious broadcasting industry. Apart from corporate owners of media outlets, no other force in society has access to such a big soapbox. Most of what emanates from the Christian TV and radio stations is the preaching of a conservative religious gospel. But in recent decades, evangelicals have broadened their notion of "the gospel" to include all sorts of ideological themes. Typically, on the Christian Right networks, several hours a day are devoted to political programming. Concerned Women for America president Beverly LaHaye broadcasts her half-hour daily radio show to an estimated audience of 500,000. Most of LaHaye's broadcasts end with action suggestions for listeners: call your Congressmember, send money to a crisis pregnancy center, find out if your school library carries one of the objectionable books named on the show.

James Dobson's Focus on the Family is the largest of the radio ministries. Syndicated daily on hundreds of radio stations, and with monthly mailings sent to more than two million supporters, Dobson covers everything from children's bedtime stories to anti-gay rights ballot initiatives. Yet the seamless ease with which Dobson and other broadcasters move from the mundane to the partisan is part of the medium's effectiveness. What attracts large and loyal audiences is the notion that everything matters. In the scheme of things, parental skill at toilet training is as pleasing to God as is a Christian's campaign for a city council seat.

Mainstream news reporting of right-wing activism, though much better than it used to be, is bound by the event-driven imperatives of journalism. News focuses on unusual actions taken by unusual people. Someone runs for office, makes an offensive speech, blockades a building or is found to have broken the law, and that makes the news. What escapes most media coverage are the routine ways and means through which the Right keeps its foot soldiers prepared to strike when it is time to vote, lobby, or protest. Most of this activity happens outside official political channels. It happens in Wednesday night church meetings and over weekday Christian call-in shows. It is evident in the pages of the, literally, scores of right-wing newsletters and magazines that circulate outside the purview of the mainstream press.

In our media culture, images and opinions based often on little more than sound bites can make or break a campaign. As image makers and opinion shapers, the Right uses a range of cultural means—from popular video tapes to computer bulletin boards to Promise Keepers men's rallies—to communicate with supporters in language that supersedes the nuts-and-bolts of politics itself.

In these essays, I aim to present some of the complexity of what makes the Right work. Some of the articles focus on right-wing think tanks, analyzing their roles in shaping and/or granting legitimacy to government policies. Other selections focus more on the grassroots activism conducted by the Christian Right. My goal has been to give readers a sense of what makes a social movement successful. The numerous names and details help tell the stories, and together they map the diversity of projects and players on the Right. These articles are descriptive because my goal has been to provide continuous, written documentation of events and trends as they unfold. The articles were written for particular alternative press outlets and, therefore, conform to the time and space constraints I was under. Most of the articles were originally published in the monthly *Z magazine*, whose editors gave me free reign to write articles as long as I wanted. A few of the selections appeared in a column I wrote for a brief time for the *Humanist* magazine. Others were written originally as short news articles for the now-defunct but once venerable *Guardian* newspaper.

Many of the articles are reports from the right-wing conferences I cannot seem to stay away from. Others are based on interviews with activists and my reading of the right-wing press. Over the years, I have developed some reliable, though time-consuming methods for studying the Right. I rely mostly on what scholars call "primary source" materials, rather than the second-hand reports of other writers. Since the early 1980s, I have subscribed to about 100 right-wing periodicals. Some of these are available free-of-charge once one gets on the right mailing lists; most I pay for. These include a wide range of materials: popular evangelical magazines such as *Charisma* and *Christianity Today*, the weekly conservative *Human Events* newspaper and William F. Buckley's biweekly *National Review* magazine, the Liberty Lobby's weekly *Spotlight* newspaper, about a dozen regional conservative Christian newspapers, and scores of newsletters from think tanks, missionary strategists, white supremacist groups, conspiracy theorists—ad infinitum. I supplement this goldmine with regular monitoring of Christian TV and radio broadcasts. Through the broadcasts and periodicals, I learn about upcoming conferences, and I attend as many as possible, under my real name.

The articles in this collection are organized in an obvious way. In the 1990s, the Christian Right has been the largest and most influential of right-wing movements. The first section begins with reportage from the Christian Coalition's 1995 national conference. From there the collection includes profiles of many Christian Right groups and activities, intended to convey how the movement successfully combines electoral and cultural politics.

Section II of the book groups together coverage of a number of secular right-wing projects, beginning with two articles on the National Association of Scholars which, in the early 1990s, led the charge against "political correctness" in the universities.

This section lifts its title "Ideas Have Consequences" from a famous 1950s book by the same name, written by a prominent conservative intellectual, Richard Weaver. He and others of his era urged the Right to concentrate their efforts on building cultural and ideological institutions. "Ideas have consequences" later became the motto of the Heritage Foundation. In this section I include a number of articles on the influence of right-wing think tanks, on everything from foreign and military policy to anti-environmentalism to the mass media. I also include here an article on organizations active against Mexican immigrants. For part of the Right, xenophobia is central to their brand of anti-establishment patriotism.

In the third section on the patriot movement, I include a couple of articles on the electoral politics of groups outside of dominant right-wing circles, namely the Liberty Lobby and the U.S. Taxpayers Party, both of which represent themselves as "populists." The mid-1990s saw the rise of armed right-wing militias, which grew in part out of the earlier tax protest and white supremacist movements. In Part III I include two articles that predated the militia phenomenon plus two written in the wake of the Oklahoma City bombing. A subset of the patriot movement, the militias require much more research and analysis before their definitive story can be told.

* * *

The sheer scope of right-wing movement activity appears overwhelming and, in many respects, it is. The Left has nothing to compete with the Right's multibillion dollar organizational infrastructure. Funding for the think tanks and many media projects comes from corporate foundation donors, but the grassroots Christian Right is funded mostly by the hundreds of thousands of regular folks who send twenty dollars here and one hundred dollars there. The Right has succeeded through a combination of abundant resources, the dedication of movement participants and some of the advantages afforded by our existing political system.

The Christian Right, for example, has won elected offices and influence within the Republican Party largely because of persistent low voter turnout. Several years ago the Christian Coalition calculated that if only thirty percent of the eligible electorate goes to the polls, then it takes only fifteen percent plus one percent to win any race. Sometimes this strategy has failed, as when informed voters have rejected previously elected Christian Right candidates. But by default, well-organized minorities can reap windfalls when most everyone else declines to participate. This is one of the secrets to the Right's success.

Decades ago, the massive civil rights movement defeated the large, well-organized and well-financed segregationist movement by working both within and outside of the existing power structure. Next, the anti-war and women's movements similarly combined tactics of both an electoral and cultural nature. In all three of these cases, as in the cases of right-wing social movements, success has come in small doses and only through the kind of collective energy one might harness to move a mountain.

This sounds dismal now. At present one cannot see on the horizon a progressive movement massive enough to stop the current onslaught from the Right. But that means great opportunity, not defeat. There is growth potential for the Left to learn more about how our system works, including the role of right-wing movements. Every action taken now to blunt the power of the Right and to press for humane policies is a stepping stone on the path toward an eventual respite, and a redirection of the course our country is on.

Part I
The Christian Right

The Christian Coalition

No Stop Signs
on the Road to Victory

The Nation, October 9, 1995

The afternoon before the start of this year's Christian Coalition "Road to Victory" convention, more than 300 activists packed Room 345 of the Cannon House Office Building before fanning out to lobby their Senators and Congress members. They went armed with printed lists of "talking points" on seven of the Coalition's top legislative proposals. Their assignment was to spend no more than twenty minutes in each office and then to record their legislators' responses on issues ranging from the abolition of the Department of Education and the defunding of the National Endowment for the Arts and the Corporation for Public Broadcasting to a federal ban on late-term abortions and a constitutional amendment to reinstate voluntary school prayer.

Camille Mitzner, the Coalition's grassroots legislative liaison, had scheduled 185 of these constituent visits in the week before the convention. Leaders of states with large Coalition memberships organized their own delegations, for a total of 400 citizen lobbying sessions conducted in a two and a half hour shift. Data collected on "report cards" for each of the legislators will be used to compile the Coalition's voter guides for next year's elections.

Without the efficient organizing by the Coalition's Washington, D.C., staff, those 300 activists might not have known what office door to knock on or what to say when they sat down. Without the volunteer labor of those 300 activists and thousands more who came to town the next day, at their own expense, the Coalition would not be the single largest, most formidable grassroots force active in U.S. politics.

More than 4,000 Coalition members filled the Washington Hilton hotel for the two-day convention, up from 3,000 in 1994 and 2,500 in 1993. Last year, the Coalition boasted 1,100 chapters across the country; this year the count rose to 1,700 chapters. They came not just to hear solicitous speeches from Newt Gingrich, Bob Dole, Phil Gramm, Patrick Buchanan, and Coalition leaders Pat Robertson and Ralph Reed. They came to celebrate their victories over the past year and to fortify themselves for the coming election season. They intend to throw the Democrats out of the White House, to expand the Republican majority in Congress, and to see passage of their ambitious Contract with the American Family legislation.

These are goals shared by both the Coalition leadership and its rank-and-file activists. Unity on this agenda eases an ongoing tension between the Coalition's national political strategists, who are prone to make compromises with the reigning Republicans, and the more hard-line grassroots activists, who see no gray area on issues such as abortion.

Republican presidential candidates know they must win votes from millions of the Christian Right stalwarts. That is why all but Arlen Specter and Pete Wilson made a beeline to speak at the convention. The volume of the applause and the number of standing ovations each candidate received said something about who was most favored. Lamar Alexander and Richard Lugar got cordial but lukewarm responses. Phil Gramm and Bob Dole, seen as the two most serious contenders, both rated high on the applause meter. Each used his campaign speech to proclaim himself more "pro-life" than the other, but neither of them was the crowd's favorite.

Not surprisingly, Alan Keyes, the African American talk show host and former Reagan administration ambassador to UNESCO, was a smash hit. These churchgoers thrive on exhilarating oratory, and for months Keyes has been firing up Christian Right crowds around the country with stronger anti-abortion rhetoric than any of his competitors. One Coalition member from Michigan explained to me her enthusiasm for Keyes. "Those of us who've been accused of being the most bigoted in this country, we're the ones who are flocking to him," she said. "And it's not because he's black or because he's an intellectual. It's because of the ideas he espouses."

Yet other conventioneers I spoke with worry that Keyes is a

spoiler who will take votes away from their favorite, Patrick Buchanan. Among the crowd of hundreds who greeted Buchanan in the hotel lobby before his closing night banquet speech, most of those I spoke to were undecided on whom they will vote for in the primaries. Yet it was Buchanan who brought the house down with his delivery of one-liners like the one about how the Department of Education is run by a bunch of "secular humanists in sandals and beads." Buchanan pointed out that among his rivals, Senators Dole, Gramm, Lugar and Specter had all voted to approve Supreme Court justices Ruth Bader Ginsburg and Stephen Breyer, thus solidifying the pro-choice Court for years to come. "Not by their honeyed words, but by their fruits shall ye know them," he reminded the crowd.

During the convention, one CBS news report ended with a line to the effect that while no Republican primary candidate can win the nomination without the Christian Right, that same alliance will doom the Republicans to defeat in the general election. I asked Guy Rodgers what he thought of this analysis. Rodgers is the Christian Coalition's former national field director and was, until recently, Buchanan's campaign manager. If the "pro-family" movement were truly an albatross for the Republicans at the national level, Rodgers said, then the party would have "suffered a blood bath" in 1994. The exact opposite happened, and Rodgers thinks the Buchanan campaign will successfully push both the Gramm and Dole candidacies to the right.

The abortion issue will be pivotal in this process. While anti-gay rhetoric was sparse—and unlike at last year's event, there were no anti-gay literature tables in the exhibit hall—virtually all the speakers pounded on abortion. The Christian Right worries that so-called moderate Republicans will try to remove the party's "pro-life" plank in San Diego at the Republican National Convention next August. To head off the pro-choicers, Phyllis Schlafly's Republican National Coalition for Life collects petitions from rank-and-file party members and from elected officials who pledge support to an unyielding anti-abortion party line.

But curiously, the national leadership of the Christian Coalition is suspect on this score. Last spring, executive director Ralph Reed retracted an earlier threat he had made—that the Coalition would not accept a pro-choice presidential or vice-presidential nominee. The Contract with the American Family calls for Congress "to begin the process of restoring respect for the sanctity of life of unborn children." This language reflects the Coalition's decision to lobby first for a ban on only late-term abortions. Since release of the Contract last May, harder line anti-abortion groups have charged the leadership with selling out the "pro-life" cause for political expediency. For example, the American Life League, one of the oldest and most prominent national anti-abortion groups, has been circulating a pamphlet, "Testing Rhetoric Against Reality," that blasts the Coalition for giving politicians a loophole that will let them "focus on less than one percent of the 1.5 million human beings who are killed annually by decriminalized abortion."

To forestall a likely revolt from the grassroots, the Christian Coalition seems now to have restiffened its anti-abortion stance. At the convention, Ralph Reed and Pat Robertson issued no ultimatum to candidates. Instead, they allowed Phyllis Schlafly (who called abortion "the central moral issue of our time") and other speakers to do so. Pro-life rhetoric yielded the most thunderous applause from the 4,000 assembled.

The tension within the Christian Coalition over how hard to press its social agenda is not going to go away. But as long as its leadership can convey a sense to the grassroots that they are moving forward, they may never have to confront it head-on. If anything, what keeps Coalition members unified as the years go by, in my view, is the chance to make an impact in their home towns. Each chapter has its pet projects, and members flock to annual conventions to swap success stories and to pick up new ideas.

A small group from Cut Off, Louisiana, recently stopped their school district's plan to give contraceptive information to junior high students. Bob McClellan, a San Diego county Buick dealer, Coalition organizer and El Cajon city council member, recently won Focus on the Family's "Hometown Hero of the Year" award for his role in passing a California state ban on sidewalk pornography vending machines. (The law is currently on appeal in the courts.) McClellan sponsors monthly clergy luncheons for hundreds of San Diego area pastors. He comes to the annual conventions to tell others how they can organize such recruitment meetings.

Jerry Klinkner, director of the Coalition's Chicago chapter, is working to start ten more chapters this year in Cook County, Illinois. To support his full-time time work for the cause, Klinkner handed out flyers asking Coalition members to sign up for a long-distance phone company that will direct ten percent of customers' bills to his activities.

At the convention, each speaker seemed to understand the need to balance the Coalition's reputation for organizational devotion with the sort of God talk that stirs the blood of the ones who must go back home to stuff envelopes and walk precincts. This year, noticeably more than last, the rhetoric of the speakers was heavily laden with Christian themes. Ralph Reed told the audience that "my prayer today is that as the world looks at us, they do not see Republicans or Democrats," but rather "followers of a humble carpenter from Galilee." Senator Phil Gramm closed his campaign speech with his own profession of faith. "There's only one person whose values are good enough to impose on America," Gramm said. "And when He comes back, He's not going to need the government." Patrick Buchanan ended his thundering tirade with a line about "crossing the threshold of a new millennium," and his final rallying cry: "The time is not long when we're all going to have to take that march up to Armageddon and do battle for the Lord."

With a multi-issue agenda that draws people in on matters dear to their hearts, with tried-and-true grassroots lobbying tactics, and a willingness to operate within the confines of the existing electoral party system, the Christian Coalition is unified in its goal of deciding who will sit in the White House. Failing that, though, the Christian Right will continue to seek the Kingdom—from the biggest Congressional races to the most humble school board fights. They believe they cannot lose.

The New Man

Z Magazine, December 1995

Fifty thousand men filled the Oakland, California sports coliseum and kicked off their Promise Keepers weekend men's rally by chanting: "We love Jesus, yes we do. We love Jesus. How about you?" Thus began seventeen hours' worth of hand-clapping, singing, shouting, praying, weeping and endless speeches by evangelical celebrities on the need for men to repent for neglecting their families and to, once again, take their rightful place as heads of their households.

The Oakland rally was a repeat of the Promise Keepers road show that packed stadiums in 13 cities in 1995. A total of 720,000 born-again Christian men, some travelling great distances, paid $55 each to don baseball caps and polo shirts and sit in the blazing sun for hours on end. They must have had a motive.

There was the surface level spectacle of a standing army united to some degree by a drive to reaffirm male dominance. The Promise Keepers organization, started in 1990, is growing by leaps and bounds. It is a phenomenon worth probing because it reflects what is going on within the evangelical subculture as well as how some men are, belatedly, responding to feminism.

As an event series, the Promise Keepers idea is both simple and a sure-fire draw. Legend has it that in 1990 Bill McCartney, who was then Coach of the University of Colorado football team, was driving with a friend to a meeting of the Fellowship of Christian Athletes when the two hit on the idea of filling a sports stadium with Christian men. They held their first gathering of 4,200 men at the University of Colorado in 1991, then went national with a quarter of a million men gathering in seven sites in 1994. By 1995 the full-time staff of Promise Keepers had grown to 250, with an annual budget of $64 million.

There are some obvious keys to the success of Promise Keepers. The events bring men to familiar local sports stadiums, where they can eat hot dogs and feel like it's just another day at the game with the guys. The speakers all dress and talk like peppy coaches. Most of the speakers are well-known evangelical leaders, including some who have been regulars on Christian TV and radio shows for years: Bill Bright of Campus Crusade for Christ, Luis Palau, Franklin Graham (son of Billy), Pastors Jack Hayford, E.V. Hill, T.D. Jakes and Raul Ries.

The Promise Keepers events are promoted relentlessly through Christian media. This past summer, KFAX radio in the San Francisco area, along with 400 other radio stations, broadcast a 90-second "Men of Action Radio Highlight" every weekday afternoon. The popular monthly *Charisma* magazine, with a circulation in excess of 100,000, was an early promoter. In 1994, *Charisma*'s publisher Stephen Strang started *New Man*, the Promiser Keepers' own glossy bimonthly magazine; circulation: 500,000. *New Man* is full of easy-to-read stories about Christian athletes, happy marriages, and churches that foster inter-racial friendships. Promise Keepers brings out the crowds through a network of 10,000 local church coordinators. Volunteers called "Point Men" are appointed by local pastors to link Promise Keepers with church men's groups. Volunteer "Ambassadors" are recruited to introduce Promise Keepers to clergy and to encourage them to start a men's ministry connected with the national organization. Promise Keepers does not compete with the projects of a local church. At the Oakland rally and others, men came in groups from their home churches. Some blocked off areas of the stadium so they could all sit together wearing their church T-shirts.

Camp Meetings

At one level Promise Keepers is a form of cheap entertainment and a social gathering for the male division of the already converted. Promise Keepers has made front-page news in major newspapers because it looks to secular reporters like something new. (Or is it because any large assemblage of men must be inherently newsworthy?) This series of stadium events is part of a long tent revival tradition within the evangelical subculture. In the 1940s and 1950s evangelist Billy Graham made headlines when he began preaching to large rallies in major cities. In those years, newspaper magnate William Randolph Hearst and Henry Luce of *Time* magazine gave Graham fawning press coverage because Graham was a strident anticommunist.

Graham continues to draw the multitudes, as do countless other preachers one rarely reads about in the secular press. The "Jesus freak" movement of the early 1970s was built through mass rallies and Christian rock concerts, some of which went on for days. Currently leaders of the charismatic movement are embroiled in a controversy over something called "holy laughter." Preachers of this phenomenon persuade the audience to experience the "gifts of the Holy Spirit" by falling to the floor and letting loose with wild laughter, sometimes for hours at a time.

Promise Keepers is a variation on the tent revival. Its goal is to revitalize evangelical churches, with a particular bent on male "leadership" and "racial reconciliation." Despite the male pastorate in evangelical churches, women attend and participate in far greater numbers. (Women are also overrepresented among Christian TV and radio audiences.) Promise Keepers is in part an effort to get hubby excited about going to church more often and to tap his unused time and energy for all sorts of missionary and possibly political projects.

There is also an economic incentive. Christian book publishing is a multi-billion dollar a year industry. Just in the past few years, Christian book stores have cleared shelf space for new "men's issues" sections stocked with titles such as *A Man's Work is Never Done*, *The Man in the Mirror*, and *Tender Warrior*.

"Racial reconciliation" is a major theme for Promise Keepers as it is now for most of the evangelical movement. This is something many progressives are loathe to recognize, because they would prefer to cast evangelicals as uniformly racist. But after decades of segregation in the churches, it is the most conservative white denominations that have, for the past several years, been publicly repenting for church racism, and forging new alliances with Black church leaders. The secular press has largely ignored this story, even though it has implications for the Christian Right's goal of racially integrating its ranks.

The Christian Coalition invites panels of African American

speakers to its annual conferences, though this tokenism is not yet matched by more than a handful of people of color who attend Coalition events. But since the late 1980s, the guest lists and hosts of Christian TV shows have become increasingly integrated. *Charisma* magazine has published a series of articles on racial reconciliation, including a June 1995 article that was favorable toward inter-racial marriage. Rhetoric around "racial reconciliation" typically does not mention the political-economic roots of racial injustice. Instead, racism is portrayed as a sin of prejudice among individuals. Still, racial reconciliation offers great growth potential for church builders and for the Christian Right, which wants to absolve itself of the racist stereotype and enlist Black and Latino conservatives who oppose abortion, gay rights and affirmative action.

Promise Keepers is playing an important role in the racial reconciliation project. Men who attend the stadium rallies pledge themselves to uphold "seven promises." These include obeying the Bible; "practicing spiritual, moral, ethical, and sexual purity," i.e., no extra-marital fooling around; and "building strong marriages and families." Promise #6 is to reach "beyond any racial and denominational barriers to demonstrate the power of biblical unity." The Promise Keepers rallies all feature Black and Latino speakers. The crowds are mostly white men, but they are being inculcated in the virtues of crossing racial lines for a shared "family values" agenda.

Leaders and Servants

As an organization, Promise Keepers itself backs no partisan agenda. However, the group's politics are evident. Founder Bill McCartney has been a board member of Colorado for Family Values, which sponsored that state's 1992 anti-gay rights ballot measure. The event at the Oakland coliseum included an exhibit hall of "ministry booths." Organizations ranged from Christian father-and-son campout groups to well-known missionary agencies to the more overtly partisan. Focus on the Family, which publishes *The Seven Promises of a Promise Keeper*, was on hand as was the affiliated Washington, D.C.-based Family Research Council think tank. Exodus International, the country's leading "ministry" to counsel gays and lesbians out of their "lifestyle," was there with pamphlets from a slew of local anti-gay church groups.

There was no political hard sell, but the message was uniformly conservative. There were no ministries for "men of integrity" who want to help men in poverty. No Sermon on the Mount stuff for these Christians.

Yet they use Jesus as their role model as it suits them. The Oakland rally was preceded by a heavily attended press conference. Coach McCartney was asked about Promise Keepers' incessant talk about "male leadership." McCartney's canned response, repeated by Promise Keepers president Randy Phillips, was that when they say "leadership," they intend the word in a Biblical context, meaning "servanthood." Christ led by serving his disciples. Therefore, Promise Keepers need to go home and be "servants" for their wives and kids. By dodging and weaving around "leadership" and "servanthood," Promise Keepers may encourage men to do more chores around the house. But the role model, Christ, is still King of Kings.

McCartney and Phillips were trying to maneuver the press away from the impression that Promise Keepers promotes crude, old-fashioned sexism. The impression comes through in some of the literature circulated at Promise Keepers rallies, despite the rhetorical wiggling about "servanthood."

One of the regular speakers, an African American preacher named Tony Evans, circulated a newsletter from his Urban Alternative ministry in Dallas. Evans writes that "American men are increasingly allowing themselves to be 'sissified'.... I must lay the burden of the demise of our community and our culture directly in the hands of the feminized male.... We are raising a generation of passive men—a generation of men who are going to raise boys that become effeminate wife beaters. We are raising boys who will beat their wives because that's the only way they can get control." To head off this disaster, Evans tells men that if they want to "reclaim" their manhood, they must start at home, not by asking their wives to let them have their leadership role back, but by simply demanding it.

There is no way to know how many Promiser Keepers are

drawn precisely by this tough-guy talk. For some, Promise Keepers may be nothing less than a last ditch effort to feel the rush of male aggression directed toward women. Others, I suspect, are trying to create for themselves a new male identity, within a religious subculture that is male supremacist to the core. The "new man" may be some sort of hybrid, a mix of John Wayne, Alan Alda and Billy Graham, ready to "serve" as long as he can also still "lead." Promise Keepers allows men a place where they can still be "men only," where they can cry and repent for their sins without feeling too girlish because they are, after all, in a stadium with "the Coach."

In the real world, even Promise Keepers must cope with a society increasingly less tolerant of brutish men at the workplace and in politics. Like it or not, feminism has changed the way even the most fundamentalist women relate to their husbands. The economy demands that many take wage-paying jobs, and they cannot help but notice that other women succeed when they demand to be treated as equals. Even the Christian Coalition relies heavily on women chapter leaders and paid organizers. Inside their own four walls, the Promise Keepers may still reign supreme, but somehow even these good ol' boys must live with the idea that women are more than doormats.

Abortion Politics

Z Magazine, May 1995

On abortion, both the Republicans and the Christian Right have painted themselves into a corner. The party is now dependent on the Christian Right, its sole mass-based electoral constituency. The movement turns out millions of loyal Republican voters and provides the vital activists who run GOP county committees, walk precincts and deliver voter guides. At the national level the faction of so-called moderate Republicans worry that they cannot win the presidency in 1996 unless they can credibly hold an echelon of Republican voters who are turned off by the Christian Right's moral legislative agenda.

Some leaders of the Christian Right tried to cement their ties to the Republicans by endorsing a handful of pro-choice "moderate" Republicans last year. That strategy threatened to cause havoc among the movement's grassroots activists, for whom there can be no compromise with "baby killers," "sodomites" and the like. To head off rebellion from below, Christian Coalition executive director Ralph Reed recently issued an ultimatum: his 1.5 million member Christian Coalition will take a hike, he said, if the party nominates a pro-choice presidential or vice-presidential candidate in 1996.

That strengthens movement unity. But Reed and some of the other same Christian Right leaders now so cozy with the Republicans want to twist and turn further on abortion. They want to keep up the drum beat about "abortuaries" and a fetal "holocaust." Then they want to deny all responsibility for helping to fuel the violent wing of the anti-abortion movement. Each new attack on doctors and clinic workers raises the public relations liability for Republicans hooked on Christian Right support. Yet each time the most respectable leaders of the Christian Right condemn the clinic shootings and bombings, they intensify the desperation of the "justifiable homicide" advocates among them.

Signs of the Times

It was a sign of the Christian Right's growing political power when, on the heels of the 1994 Congressional election, Clinton fired Surgeon General Joycelyn Elders. She had uttered the dreaded word "masturbation" in public. But her remark was just one in a long series of forthright statements about sexual tolerance and public health. Clinton's new nominee, Dr. Henry Foster, has turned out to be much worse from the Christian Right's stand point because this doctor has actually performed abortions. If, under pressure from anti-abortionists, the Senate rejects Foster's nomination, the movement will have scored one more victory. If Foster squeaks by, the Christian Right will have another atrocity to rally behind in the 1996 campaign against Clinton.

Since last November the legal-lobbying wing of the anti-abortion movement has been trumpeting the election of about 40 new "pro-life" Congressmembers and five new "pro-lifers" in the Senate. According to the National Right to Life Committee, not a single incumbent "pro-life" member of Congress was defeated by a pro-choice opponent. About 75 percent of the newly elected Republican House members and 82 percent of newly elected Senate members are "pro-life," meaning that the GOP's future success is linked at least partly to the anti-abortion cause.

Among the new Republican Congress are a group of seven anti-choice women who were elected with the help of the Susan B. Anthony List. This is a new political action committee named after the famous suffragist leader. The SBA List, just started in 1994, gave $50,000 to eleven right-wing women candidates. The seven winners were: Helen Chenoweth (R-ID), Barbara Cubin (R-WY), Sue Myrick (R-NC), Andrea Seastrand (R-CA), Linda Smith (R-WA), Barbara Vucanovich (R-NV), and Enid Waldholtz (R-UT).

The consolidation of an informal anti-abortion Congressional caucus spells disunity for the party. Already a group of so-called moderate Republicans had to oppose a $17 billion spending cut bill because the anti-abortionists attached to it an amendment that would have allowed states to deny Medicaid-funded abortions for victims of rape or incest. It seems that a moderate Republican is one who can vote, with a clear conscience, to take food from the mouths of living children. But cutting aid to abortion-seeking women who "didn't ask for it" is too much.

A more publicized debate has been the one about whether welfare limits under the Contract with America will cause more young women to choose abortion. Some of the less partisan anti-abortion leaders, including Archbishop John Cardinal O'Connor and Helen Alvare who represents the National Council of Catholic Bishops, oppose welfare cuts on the grounds that they may increase abortion rates. The Christian Coalition and the Family Research Council, organizations more consistently aligned with the party, want to scrap welfare because they claim it subsidizes a "culture of illegitimacy and dependency." If single women can't raise their kids alone, let them go join churches that will help them.

The strategy of the Christian Coalition in particular has been to help the GOP legislate its economic program, not just in hopes of future pay-back on the moral issues but also because the Christian Right generally supports brutal capitalism. Economic issues tend to unify the Right which is why, in the early 1980s, the Reaganites focused on tax cuts and militarism and did little to appease the Christian Right on abortion and school prayer. Betrayed by the administration they helped elect, evangelical activists spent the 1980s building influence at the local grassroots level, which is why they now command great influence within the party.

Now movement leaders like Focus on the Family's Dr. James Dobson can write credibly, as he did in a January 1995 letter to supporters, that "there are millions of voters who will look elsewhere for candidates if the party abandons the unborn child.... We're expecting more from the party in control of Congress than economic and governmental reform.... If the Republicans fail to address the things that matter most, I believe a third party will coalesce around an emphatically pro-life candidate in '96."

No Place to Hide

The failure of the Reagan-Bush administration to deliver on its anti-abortion promises seemed to trigger the rash of clinic bombings beginning around 1984. As the attacks mounted, Randall Terry and others came up with the idea of Operation Rescue which began blockading clinics in early 1988. Here was a way for the movement's most aggressive members to demonstrate their commitment without getting into too much trouble. But as the jail sentences got longer and the fines bigger, and as some massive OR blockades were met with larger numbers of pro-choice people, OR started losing its momentum. "Rescuers" began to see mere civil disobedience as ineffective. Within a couple of years OR and its spin-offs started their "No Place to Hide" tactics of targeting doctors personally with "wanted" posters.

The March 1993 assassination of Dr. David Gunn inspired a tiny number of anti-abortionists to come out of the woodwork and condone "justifiable homicide." At a time when the Clinton administration had staked out a clear pro-choice position, violent anti-abortionists made the leap from debating justifiable property damage to justifiable murder. In the two years since the Gunn murder, several small-circulation publications and organizations have distinguished themselves as endorsers of the justifiable homicide line. In 1993, about two dozen individuals signed a "Defensive Action" statement drafted by Paul Hill to the effect that killing abortion doctors was justified.

Among the signers were editors of *Life Advocate*, a full-sized monthly magazine published by the Portland-based Advocates for Life. The magazine publishes both sides of the debate on killing abortion providers, and the editors themselves are careful to say that they do not personally advocate murder. But the magazine caters to activists bent on a range of harassment tactics. Each issue reports on particular clinics and doctors, with seedy looking photos taken at long distance or by amateur photographers.

One recent issue profiled Life Dynamics Inc., run by a Texan named Mark Crutcher. Life Dynamics is a three-pronged project. Crutcher uses press and local health department reports, plus all manner of clinic surveillance and infiltration, to compile potentially incriminating data on doctors and clinics. He recruits "post-abortive" women who might want to sue doctors for medical malpractice, and he says he has a list of 600 personal injury attorneys on call for possible lawsuits. LDI brags that it uses "spies, counterspies, provocateurs, disinformation, and misdirection to ferret out information on abortionists and clinics." Last year Crutcher and associates posed as something called Project Choice and convinced the National Coalition of Abortion Providers to let them do a nationwide survey of abortion doctors' views on the profession. There is no telling how much personal information Life Dynamics culled about abortion providers.

Also a signer of Paul Hill's Defensive Action statement was Dave Leach of Des Moines, Iowa. Leach publishes the *Prayer and Action Weekly News*. This is a mimeographed and amateurish little newsletter but one that serves as a key outlet for letters from and interviews with John Brockhoeft, Shelley Shannon, Paul Hill and others doing jail time for bombing clinics and shooting doctors.

Between them *Life Advocate* and *Prayer and Action Weekly News* are sort of an underground press for the justifiable homicide gang. Violent anti-abortionists are using these and related publications to debate and hone their arguments in favor of killing. *Life Advocate* has advertised a new book called *A Time to Kill* by Michael Bray, a Lutheran minister living in Maryland. Bray spent about four years in prison for destroying seven clinics in the Washington, D.C., area.

Bray's book *A Time to Kill* is not the same as the informally circulated "Army of God" manual which details how to use guns, explosives and butyric acid. Bray's book is not tactical. It presents two central arguments for justifiable homicide and then goes back and forth between them. The first argument is that capital punishment is called for in the Bible. The state is responsible for punishing people guilty of capital offenses. But because the state is now in the business of helping doctors get away with murder, it's OK for believers to conduct their own extra-judicial executions. The second argument is the "defense of necessity." Individual "pro-lifers" have the right to get up in the morning and go "prevent" a doctor from killing unborn children that day. Both arguments are presented in rational-sounding language laced with lots of Bible quotes. Bray stresses that to be "pro-life" is not to be "pacifist," and that anyone who says otherwise must not really believe that fetuses are human. In his newsletter *Capitol Area Christian News*

Bray routinely trashes Operation Rescue leaders Flip Benham, Pat Mahoney and Randall Terry, all of whom have publicly rejected justifiable homicide.

Randall Terry has been writing lately in the Christian press to the effect that it is the Freedom of Access to Clinic Entrances (FACE) Act that has led frustrated anti-abortionists to take up arms. "Planned Parenthood, NARAL, the NOW and the rest of the abortion industry can partly blame themselves for the recent shootings," Terry writes. "They clamored for harsh treatment of pro-lifers and they usually got it. Now they have to deal with the violent fringe." Of course, this claim is ludicrous, as FACE was passed only in 1994, after a decade of escalating violence.

Facing the Music

Terry and others seem to want to unite their splintering movement around opposition to FACE, and they have planned a number of demonstrations to defy the law. Currently anti-abortion forces are breaking up into roughly three factions: the legal legislative wing, which was never keen on direct action, including the National Right to Life Committee and Judie Brown's American Life League; Operation Rescue leaders who publicly renounce violence; and the still small but growing faction of justifiable homicide endorsers.

The FACE law is a wedge between the factions. Clinic attacks are now a federal crime, and the Justice Department has recently subpoenaed pro- and anti-violence activists for secretive grand jury-type interrogations. Either the government can collect testimony proving a nationwide conspiracy to commit violence, which is unlikely; or the government can go through the motions to satisfy the liberal pressure groups calling for a broad crackdown on anti-abortion groups.

In any event, application of FACE is exacerbating factionalism between fellow anti-abortionists. Recently, Kansas City radio host Regina Dinwiddie, part of the justifiable homicide faction, has been sued for allegedly violating FACE by advocating violence in public. Father David Trosch, a signer of the Paul Hill statement, is being sued under FACE for allegedly conspiring against an Alabama clinic doctor. In an appearance on a

"Geraldo Rivera" show, Trosch said that the doctor should be killed.

As of this writing, neither the American Center for Law and Justice nor the Rutherford Institute, the Christian Right's stellar law firms, have been willing to represent Dinwiddie or Trosch. The task has fallen to two pro-bono attorneys, Michael Hirsh and Vincent Heuser of Liberty and Justice, Inc. Hirsh was formerly with the ACLJ but he was quietly removed last year after he wrote an article defending justifiable homicide. The article was rejected by Pat Robertson's Regent University *Law Review* only after Hirsh's client Paul Hill killed a doctor and assistant in July.

The point is that "respectable" Christian Right organizations and leaders, having fueled the movement with ceaseless talk about "baby killers," now want no association with those who might act on such words. Yet there is no way to determine how widely acceptable the justifiable homicide line is with rank-and-file members of the Christian Right.

Michael Bray's sister-in-law Donna has a project called Defenders of the Defenders of Life which she is using in part to raise the legal fees for the Dinwiddie and Trosch cases. In a phone interview Mrs. Bray told me that her faction is a minority of the "pro-life" movement but that she has received hundreds of supportive letters since the Paul Hill shootings.

The letters-to-the-editor pages of *Life Advocate* magazine include lots of endorsements of violence. Typical of the kind of letters appearing in more mainstream evangelical newspapers was one published in the *Southern California Christian Times* after the killing of two clinic workers in Brookline. The writer finds it "abhorrent and ironic that pro-abortion spokespeople nationwide are demanding that the entire country mourn for two women who made a career of scheduling the executions of countless unborn children." She concludes by comparing abortion doctors to "violent criminals everywhere," and she warns "woe to every abortionist who, escaping justice here on earth, will stand before He who comes again to judge the living and the dead on the last day!"

Concerned Women for America, with an official membership of 600,000, is among the most influential of Christian Right groups. In a recent editorial in its *Family Voice* magazine, CWA condemned "pro-life" killers Michael Griffin, Paul Hill and John Salvi—but because their vigilante actions were "unauthorized." Christians must obey the law, CWA stressed. "Murderers of every type, including abortionists, certainly deserve the death penalty. but who has the authority to administer it? Only civil government can claim the authority to use the death penalty—not individuals."

But how thoroughly and for how long can the thousands of activists who call abortion murder obey a civil government that upholds women's right to abortion? A recent survey conducted by the evangelical *World* news magazine found that relatively few avowedly "pro-life" ministers actually preach or organize against abortion. The study was intended to show that pastors have neglected their duty. But the study also implies that anti-abortion activism, at least among Protestants, is less directed by church authorities than one might have thought.

The various factions of the anti-abortion movement are unstable and cannot be controlled by those Christian Right leaders courting favor with the Republican party. Shortly after threatening the GOP against a pro-choice 1996 presidential ticket, Christian Coalition director Ralph Reed back-pedaled and said, on a CNN talk show, that he would not want to "issue a litmus test." To do otherwise, though, threatens the Christian Coalition's credibility with its 1.5 million dues-paying members. The party cannot thrive without loyal support from the Christian Right, and the movement cannot preserve unity and purpose if it abandons the anti-abortion cause. While violent "pro-lifers" remain a threat to the public at large, the party and the movement are headed for trouble around abortion politics. They may reap what they have sown.

It's Political Power, Stupid!

Z Magazine, January 1995

Only the ostriches should be surprised. Preliminary data from exit polls indicate that about 30 percent of the people who voted in November were white evangelical Christians. Among these, about 69 percent voted Republican. There was nothing "stealth" about it. The stated agenda of the Christian Right in 1994 was to help deliver the Senate and Congress to the Republicans—and to credibly claim credit for doing just that.

The 30 percent figure means that the Christian Right is, each time around, doing a better and better job of getting its people to the polls. In the 1992 presidential election, only about 18 percent of the voters were self-identified white evangelicals. The figure for the 1990 midterm election was 15 percent.

The trend began in the late 1970s when the Christian Right registered several million new voters to vote for Ronald Reagan. In 1980, when Reagan won with only 26 percent of the eligible electorate, white evangelical voters accounted for two thirds of Reagan's ten-point lead over Jimmy Carter. Then in 1984, the Christian Right pulled out all the stops to re-elect Reagan. In 1992, despite Bush's defeat, exit poll data showed that there were only two constituencies consistently loyal to the Republican party: people with incomes over $200,000 a year, who are few in number; and the Christian Right.

The past two decades have seen a growing symbiosis between the mass movement of evangelical Christians and the Republican Party. Since the 1968 presidential election, when nearly ten million Americans voted for segregationist Alabama Governor George Wallace, the Republicans have worked to broaden the class base of their party downward. That has meant following Wallace's lead in using issues of race, crime and morality to attract white middle and lower middle class voters.

In the mid-1970s and 1980s, Gallup poll surveys showed

that one quarter to one third of the U.S. population identified itself as "born-again" evangelicals. Most of them have become politically active only in the last 15 years or so. Certainly not all are right-wing but their numbers are large and numbers win elections. In June of 1994 a *New York Times* poll revealed that about nine percent of a national sample identified themselves as part of the Christian Right.

The handwriting was on the wall for anyone who cared to read. For twenty years, leaders of the Christian Right have built one organization after another, with the avowed purpose of winning state power, i.e., the power to influence, if not dictate, public policy. Leaders of the Christian Right worked hand-in-glove with the Reagan and Bush administrations to wage murderous wars on civilians in Central America and southern Africa. Meanwhile, the North American Left cackled along with the rest of the country at the ridiculous TV preacher scandals, which diverted people's attention from the really important players in the Christian Right.

While everyone else was laughing, the Christian Right grew into the most formidable mass movement on the political scene today. We will enter the new millennium with the Christian Right in positions of state power.

The single most important, though by no means the only, movement organization is the Christian Coalition. The Coalition's September Road to Victory conference, which I attended, drew 3,000 hard core activists for two days of strategizing at the Washington, D.C., Hilton. In plenary sessions and small workshops, Coalition leaders laid out the tactical plans by which they would change the course of U.S. history through the 1994 Congressional elections. The plans made sense. It seemed clear that the Coalition knew what it was doing. That is why Republican National Committee chair Haley Barbour sent his aide Leigh Anne Metzger to tell the conventioneers, "Despite press reports, the Republican Party holds out a welcome mat to the Christian Coalition." Major GOP presidential hopefuls Dan Quayle, Senator Phil Gramm, Dick Cheney and Lamar Alexander all made early campaign stops at the conference. But it was clear from the many rank-and-file activists I spoke with for two days that the real action is at the local level.

The Coalition claims more than a million numbers, which is probably a mailing list figure. More importantly, the Coalition, since its founding in 1989, has built 1,100 local chapters in all 50 states. Some chapters hold regular meetings with a couple hundred people. Many of the chapters are headed by women, as are some of the Coalition's state branches. Each chapter includes members of multiple charismatic and Baptist churches, meaning that the outreach capability of the Coalition goes well beyond its own numerical strength which is phenomenal in its own right. In September, the Coalition sent voter registration packets to 250,000 churches. At the convention, members organized to distribute 30 million voter guides, in 300 local versions, which they successfully did in October. Christian Coalition executive director Ralph Reed explained that the voter guides allow candidates and campaigners to bypass "expensive and biased media." On one piece of paper, the Coalition makes a chart showing pictures of the Democratic and Republican candidates for Senate, Governor and Congressional seats. The chart simply lists four to six issues phrased as the Right sees them—this year they included abortion on demand; homosexuals in the military; banning ownership of legal firearms; voluntary prayer in schools; parental choice in education—along with the words "supports" or "opposes" under each candidate's picture.

The Coalition's 1,100 chapters are responsible for distributing the voter guides by identifying sympathetic churches and by finding "pro-family" voters on a one-by-one basis. Roberta Combs, state chair of the South Carolina Christian Coalition, told conventioneers how she has organized Coalition members in 60 percent of her state's electoral precincts. "You are in warfare," she said. "Politics equals people. People equals numbers. Numbers equal precincts. Get ten people to start with. Get a map, voter registration lists, church directories, other 'pro-family' lists." Correlate these lists and identify sympathetic voters street by street, Combs urged, and then go door-to-door with the Coalition's fall voter guides.Combs is typical of many Christian Right leaders. Until recently going full-time with the Coalition, she ran a successful business as an interior designer. She began working for Republicans in local elections in 1978. Then she ran the South Carolina branch of Americans for Robertson in 1988.

She put on successful fundraising affairs for the state GOP and they elected her to be their treasurer. She and her army can now take credit for electing South Carolina's new Republican Governor David Beasley.

In Pennsylvania, Christian Coalition members backed the new Republican governor Tom Ridge, one of the party's so-called moderates. Ridge is pro-choice on abortion, which caused an outcry by some in the Christian Right in Pennsylvania; they backed a minor party anti-abortion candidate named Peg Luksik. Overall, however, the Christian Coalition's strategy was to back any and all Republicans, pro-choice or not. In California they backed gubernatorial candidate Michael Huffington who was nominally pro-choice and who had also supported the removal of the ban on gay military personnel. This game is about power, not principle.

Now as we face the coming legislative onslaught of a Republican dominated Congress, people on the Left are talking about emulating the grassroots organizing tactics of the Right. This idea is sensible but one does not create a citizen lobbying apparatus overnight. For years, people in the Christian Right have learned to make their activism a regular habit. Not a week goes by that the movement's TV and radio stations plus scores of organizational newsletters don't mobilize people to call and write their elected officials. Here are people who believe in the efficacy of their own small but persistent actions. They think their individual postcards and phone calls make a difference, and they do.

During the controversy two years ago over Clinton's proposal to allow openly gay military personnel, Christian Right activists shut down the Congressional switchboard and deluged their representatives with mail. It worked, and it worked again in early 1994 when an amendment that would have required certification of home school teachers was attached to a federal education bill. Within a week, home schooling leader Mike Farris went on two nationally syndicated Christian radio talk shows and revved up the phone trees of his 37,000-member Home School Legal Defense Association. Eight hundred thousand phone calls later, only one member of Congress was willing to vote for the amendment.

Is this the kind of activity the Left could or would emulate?

Probably not, because these dramatic incidents do not occur in a vacuum. They are made possible by the day in and day out organizing the Christian Right does, and they are made possible by the network of institutions the movement has built over several decades. These institutions include a $2.5 billion a year religious broadcasting industry, a slew of independent book publishing companies, dozens of independent regional monthly newspapers, several dozen state-based think tanks that do legislative lobbying, and an array of legal firms devoted exclusively to Christian right causes. The Left has nothing even remotely comparable.

Some left media watchers have focused recently on Rush Limbaugh, an important, though easy target. Limbaugh has millions of listeners and he has played an influential role in the Clinton-bashing of the past two years. Limbaugh attracts the Left's attention because he allegedly lies with some regularity and because he's a loud-mouthed boor. He fits the image leftists have of people on the Right. But to credit the Johnny-come-lately Rush Limbaugh with the mobilization of the Right would be like claiming that the demagogic 1930s radio priest Father Charles Coughlin was responsible for the hundreds of pro-fascist organizations that flourished in the United States during the 1930s and 1940s.

Most of what goes on in right-wing broadcasting is not like the Limbaugh show. Limbaugh is a recent phenomenon, and long after his stardom passes, the Christian Right will continue to produce much subtler and effective programming.

The religious broadcasting industry began in earnest in the 1940s. Evangelicals were then working to change laws to better secure their access to the government-regulated airwaves. They also worked, during the Cold War period, to impune the patriotism of the liberal mainline churches, which never fought back. By the early 1960s Pat Robertson started the first Christian TV network. From one tiny TV station, he built a media empire that now includes the Family Channel cable network, which currently reaches into 57 million households. The viewing audience for Robertson's weekday "700 Club" program is estimated at one million. About a third of the program's content is overtly political. Throughout the 1980s, Robertson used the "700 Club" to lobby for U.S. military aid to the Contras and to the death squads in El Salvador and Guatemala. Now he uses his network to lobby against gay rights and to get out the vote for Republicans.

Christian radio is an even more pervasive medium. There are about 1,200 full-time Christian radio stations in the United States. After country music and what is called "adult contemporary" music, Christian broadcasting stations are the most popular form of the radio medium. Standard fare on a typical Christian radio station—there are three I can listen to here in the Bay area—includes a few hours a day of political talk shows mixed in with music and inspirational teaching. KFAX in the Bay area plays James Dobson's interview show twice daily along with the weekday Concerned Women for America broadcast, which in only four years on the air has built an estimated audience of 500,000. Host Beverly LaHaye routinely uses the program to get her listeners to lobby Congress. On the hour, KFAX broadcasts the "Family News in Focus" spot, a mini-newscast of items of concern to the Christian Right. At 3:00 p.m. we get the daily commentary of Gary Bauer's Family Research Council, and by the late afternoon, there is an hour-long talk show, usually of a political nature. Christian radio is popular because it gives people emotional sustenance along with the news, traffic reports and what they need to know to be politically active.

It is the coherence of the Christian Right's cultural institutions and ideological message that makes millions of people want to participate. I have met hundreds of these people, and on a personal level, most are not the monsters they are made out to be. It is their politics we must oppose, not their quirky religious beliefs nor their right to be involved in the political process.

This is a political movement built on the foundation of some very tightly held religious views. We need to understand—note, I am not saying embrace—the religious sentiments of our fellow citizens. For evangelical Christians, one of the most politically relevant tenets is the idea that they are being persecuted by secular society. Sacrifice and martyrdom are essential themes of the Christian faith. Translated into right-wing politics the theme enables people to claim that queers and other minorities are somehow attacking the dominant culture when they demand equality. We have the most powerful political movement in the country continually claiming to be persecuted by "the Left," which the Right defines as the Clinton administration and centrist lobbies like People for the American Way. It is illogical, but the religious persecution theme keeps activists mobilized and enables them to feel comfortable about trying to deprive other people of their civil rights.

Average people active in the Christian Right feel genuinely that the country is going to hell in a handbasket, which is true. The problem is that through a long process of ideological formation most have arrived at a distorted view of their own best interests. They look at the stagnant economy and see "illegal aliens," not runaway capitalism, which they generally support. They look at teenage delinquency and then blame teachers' unions instead of the consumer culture that trains young people to shop and not to think.

What people in the Christian Right want is pretty basic. They want laws to outlaw abortion, which they consider a form of infanticide. They want to change the tax code to encourage married mothers to stay home and raise good kids. They want queers to get back in the closet and pretend not to exist. They want high quality schools; they think the public schools are failing not for lack of resources but because kids can't pray or read Genesis in biology class.

The Christian Right wants these and related things so badly that they began organizing a long time ago to win the political power necessary to change the direction of public policy. Early on, the Republican Party realized that it could become the majority party by hitching its sails to the evangelical mass movement. For two decades, the Democrats stood idly by, unwilling and unable to respond because Democrats will challenge neither the prerogatives of big business nor the ideological premises that keep people from challenging class, racial and gender inequality.

Unfortunately, the real Left, battered down by external repression and its own internal foibles, has not responded either. The Left has been unidimensionally focused on the atrocities waged at the highest levels of state power, and has been unwilling to recognize that significant numbers of our fellow citizens are decidedly reactionary. In places where fascism has taken hold, it has been through a convergence of state and corporate power with a mass base of reaction. We saw this vividly in Chile in the 1970s. I am not suggesting that our country will face a military coup. Now in the era of "democracy," from Nicaragua to the former Soviet republics, elections are the primary means through which the Right takes power. In many ways, it is already too late, though it is never really over until it's over.

Dominion Theology

Z Magazine, February 1995

The Christian Right's recent role in delivering Congress to the Republicans raises the question of just how much power the movement hopes to amass. Ralph Reed of the Christian Coalition says repeatedly that his organization wants nothing more than a representative voice in government, "a place at the table," as he puts its. Other movement leaders are more sweeping in their calls to make ours a Christian nation, a Kingdom of God on earth.

As we assess the Christian Right's future prospects, the movement's political theology is one big piece of the puzzle. Included in the movement are people with diverse viewpoints on the degree and means through which Christians ought to "take dominion" over every aspect of society. The motto of the secular Heritage Foundation, taken from the title of an influential conservative book of the 1950s, is "ideas have consequences." Yet in the past few years, with the growth in public awareness of the Christian Right, the movement's variant forms of dominion theology have attracted only scant attention.

Most of the attention has come from a new crop of researchers working on the Christian Right. Most of these people are political liberals who seek to shore up the prevailing "two-party" system by portraying their opponents—in this case, those of the Right—as aberrations on the U.S. political landscape. Liberals' writing about the Christian Right's take-over plans has generally taken the form of conspiracy theory. Instead of analyzing the subtle ways in which political ideas take hold within movements and why, the liberal conspiracy theorists use a guilt-by-association technique that goes like this: We know that a particular Christian Right author or activist has advocated bad ideas, like killing queers or forming armed militias. Then we look to see who else appears in proximity to the offender on organizational letterhead stationery or on the speakers list at movement conferences. This approach may indicate the degree of tolerance of extremist views within a given network of the broader Christian

Right movement. But the approach implies that ideas are somehow contagious: If someone serves on a board of advisors with someone else, they must think similarly and therefore be likely to behave similarly. This is the approach the Right has used to red-bait the civil rights movement, the New Left and, recently, the environmental movement.

Conspiracy theorizing about the Christian Right's supposedly "secret" agenda involves highlighting the hate-mongering and bizarre ideas of a handful of Christian Right players while neglecting the broad popularity of dominion theology. There are a variety of ideological tendencies within the Christian Right. At the truly extreme end of the spectrum is a set of ideas proponents call Reconstructionism, associated with only a small number of think tanks and book publishers. Many Christian Right activists have never even heard of Reconstructionism, whose advocates call for the imposition of an Old Testament style theocracy, complete with capital punishment for offenses including adultery, homosexuality and blasphemy.

Sects and Schisms

More prevalent on the Christian Right is the dominionist idea, shared by Reconstructionists, that Christians alone are Biblically mandated to occupy all secular institutions until Christ returns—and there is no consensus on when that might be. Dominionist thinking precludes coalitions between believers and unbelievers, which is why many Christian rightists will have a hard time compromising with some of the very same Republicans they recently helped elect.

The idea of taking dominion over secular society gained widespread currency with the 1981 publication of evangelical philosopher Francis Schaeffer's book *A Christian Manifesto*. The book sold 290,000 copies in its first year, and it remains one of the movement's most frequently cited texts. Schaeffer, who died of cancer in 1984, was a product of the internecine conflicts that split the Presbyterian church during the 1930s and 1940s. Schaeffer allied himself with the strident anticommunist leader Rev. Carl McIntire who headed the fundamentalist American Council of Christian Churches. Later Schaeffer joined an anti-

McIntire faction that, after several name changes, merged into the Presbyterian Church in America. (A related denomination, the Orthodox Presbyterian Church, is the milieu out of which convicted killer Paul Hill developed his justifications for killing abortionists.) In the 1960s and 1970s, Schaeffer and his wife Edith ran a retreat center in Switzerland, where young American "Jesus freaks" came to study the Bible with Schaeffer and learn how to apply his dominion theology to the political scene back home.

In *A Christian Manifesto*, Schaeffer's argument is simple. The United States began as a nation rooted in Biblical principles. But as society became more pluralistic, with each new wave of immigrants, proponents of a new philosophy of secular humanism gradually came to dominate debate on policy issues. Since humanists place human progress, not God, at the center of their considerations, they pushed American culture in all manner of ungodly directions, the most visible results of which included legalized abortion and the secularization of the public schools. At the end of *A Christian Manifesto*, Schaeffer called for Christians to use civil disobedience to restore Biblical morality, which explains Schaeffer's popularity with groups like Operation Rescue. Randall Terry has credited Schaeffer as a major influence in his life.

In the 1980s, some of the younger men Schaeffer had influenced joined a group called the Coalition on Revival (COR), founded by Jay Grimstead. Grimstead, a veteran of the old Young Life missionary group, had decided that evangelicals were insufficiently literalist in their reading of the Bible. Grimstead founded COR with two purposes. One was to unify pastors who differed on questions of "eschatology," which is the study of the end-times and the question of when Christ will return. Most evangelicals have held the pre-millennialist belief that Christ will return before a 1,000 year reign by believers. Grimstead and others in COR are post-millennialists who believe their job is establish the kingdom of God on earth now; Christ will return only after Christians have been in charge for 1,000 years. COR's second purpose, consistent with post-millennialism, was the development of position papers, called "world view documents," on how to apply dominion theology to Christian Right activism in more than a dozen spheres of social life, including education, economics, law and even entertainment.

Much of the liberal writing on dominion theology and Reconstructionism has focused on COR as headquarters for a conspiracy to take over society. Grimstead and his colleagues advocated running stealth candidates in selected counties as early as 1986. But in recent years, COR has served as little more than a clearinghouse for Grimstead's position papers. As an organization, COR is largely inactive. Like the Moral Majority of the early 1980s, COR was a network of pastors, each of whom is busy with his own projects.

If COR had any effect, though, it was in reinforcing ideas about taking dominion. The 100 or so movement leaders in COR each signed a "covenant" statement affirming their commitment to the idea that Christians should take dominion over all fields of secular society. Only a few of COR's steering committee members were hard core Reconstructionists. Most of the Reconstructionists are too hair-splittingly sectarian to want to associate with COR's diverse crew of pentecostal-charismatics and fundamental Baptists.

The Reconstructionists are theologically committed to Calvinism. They shy away from the Baptists' loud preaching and the pentecostals' wild practices of speaking in tongues, healing and delivering prophecies. To secular readers, the minutiae of who believes what—or which group of characters likes to dance on one foot—might seem trivial. But some of the details and divisions of Christian Right theology are politically relevant.

As Above, So Below

Reconstructionism is the most intellectually grounded, though esoteric, brand of dominion theology. Its leading proponent has been Rousas John (R.J.) Rushdoony, an obscure figure within the Christian Right. Born in 1916, the son of Armenian immigrants to the U.S., Rushdoony looks like an Old Testament patriarch with his white hair and beard and penetrating eyes. At a young age Rushdoony was strongly influenced by Westminster Theological Seminary professor Cornelius Van Til, a Dutch theologican who emphasized the inerrant authority of the Bible and the irreconcilability between believers and unbelievers. A recent issue of Rushdoony's monthly *Chalcedon Report* noted his Armenian background. Since the year 320, every generation of the Rushdoony family has produced a Christian priest or minister. "There was Armenian royalty in the Rushdoony blood, and a heritage of defending the faith, often by sword and gun, against Godless foes bent on destroying a people of faith and works."

With that auspicious heritage, Rushdoony founded the Chalcedon Foundation in California in the mid-1960s. One of the Foundation's early associates was Gary North who eventually married Rushdoony's daughter. North had been active within secular libertarian and anticommunist organizations, particularly those with an anti-statist bent.

Rushdoony and North had a falling out and ceased collaboration years ago. North started his own think tank, the Institute for Christian Economics in Tyler, Texas. Rushdoony, North and about a half dozen other Reconstructionist writers have published countless books and journals advocating postmillennialism and "theonomy" or the application of God's law to all spheres of everyday life. In his rhetorical crusades against secular humanists and against most other Christians, North is fond of saying "You can't beat something with nothing."

North has geared his writing for popular audiences; some of his books are available in Christian book stores. Rushdoony's writing is more turgid and also more controversial. It was Rushdoony's seminal 1973 tome *The Institutes of Biblical Law* that articulated Reconstructionists' vision of a theocracy in which Old Testament law would be reinstated in modern society. Old Testament law classified a wide range of sins as punishable by death; these included not only murder and rape but also adultery, incest, homosexuality, witchcraft, incorrigible delinquency by youth and even blasphemy. In the Reconstructionists' vision of a millennial or "kingdom" society, there would be only local governments; there would be no central administrative state to collect property taxes, nor to provide education or other welfare services.

Aside from Rushdoony and North, Reconstructionism boasts only a few other prolific writers. These include Dr. Greg Bahnsen, Rev. Joseph Morecraft, David Chilton, Gary DeMar and Kenneth Gentry, none of whom are major figures within the

Christian Right. They are quoted more often in liberal reports than in the Christian Right's own literature.

The unabashed advocacy of a Christian theocracy has insured a limited following for the most explicit of the Reconstructionists, who have also been sectarian in their sharp criticism of evangelicals. North, for example, has published a series of attacks on believers in the pre-millennialist version of when Christ will come back.

Perhaps even more than the punitive legal code they propose, it is the Reconstructionists' religion of Calvinism that makes them unlikely to appeal to most evangelicals. Calvinism is the by now almost archaic belief that God has already preordained every single thing that happens in the world. Most importantly, even one's own salvation or condemnation to hell is already a done deal as far as God is concerned. By this philosophical scheme, human will is not involved in changing the course of history. All that is left for the "righteous" to do is to play out their pre-ordained role, including their God-given right to dominate everyone else. Calvinism arose in Europe centuries ago in part as a reaction to Roman Catholicism's heavy emphasis on priestly authority and on salvation through acts of penance. One of the classic works of sociology, Max Weber's *Protestant Ethic and the Spirit of Capitalism*, links the rise of Calvinism to the needs of budding capitalists to judge their own economic success as a sign of their preordained salvation. The rising popularity of Calvinism coincided with the consolidation of the capitalist economic system. Calvinists justified their accumulation of wealth, even at the expense of others, on the grounds that they were somehow destined to prosper. It is no surprise that such notions still find resonance within the Christian Right which champions capitalism and all its attendant inequalities.

The hitch comes in the Calvinists' unyielding predestinarianism, the cornerstone of Reconstructionism and something at odds with the world view of evangelical Christians. Last fall in Sacramento some of the local Reconstructionists held their annual Reformation Bible Conference, cosponsored by the Covenant Reformed Church and the Chalcedon Foundation. The theme of the weekend was Christian "apologetics," meaning defense of the faith against heretical enemies of all stripes.

R.J. Rushdoony was the keynote speaker and the main draw for the 250 people in attendance. Rushdoony's message was that "any compromise with creationism is a compromise with the faith." By that he meant that all Christians must subscribe to the literal six-day creation story in the book of Genesis. Creationism, he said, means "that all power in all creation comes from above." To believe otherwise is to succumb to Darwin's theory that all power rises from, or evolves, from below. Generations before Darwin, Rushdoony said, the theory of revolution, not just evolution, gained ground through the practices of paganism and witchcraft—egalitarian religions—and the very idea that power grows from the bottom up. This (r)evolutionary heresy leads to the idea that politics, even the state, can solve human problems. No, Rushdoony insisted, "the God who created all things has thereby ordained and predestined all things."

Other speakers echoed this message. They indicted any and all fellow Christians (including the late Francis Schaeffer) who think there is a legitimate role for independent human will, let alone pluralist cooperation with unbelievers in a democracy.

The problem is that evangelicals (a category including pentecostal-charismatics and fundamental Baptists) believe that God's will works in conjunction with free human will. They believe that salvation is not by the grace of God only but by the faith of individual believers who freely choose to surrender to Jesus. In fact, the cornerstone of the Western religions is the view that God's will and human will work together. Evangelicals believe strongly that humans freely choose sin or salvation and that those already converted have the duty to go out and offer the choice they have made to others. Calvinism, in contrast, undercuts the whole motivation for missionary work, and it is the missionary zeal to redeem sinners that motivates much of the Christian Right's political activism. Calvinism is an essentially reckless doctrine. If God has already decided what's going to happen, then the dominionists do not have to take responsibility for their actions. (They can kill abortion doctors "knowing" it is the right thing to do.) Evangelicals, even those on the Right, still believe they as individuals are capable of error.

Furthermore, the Calvinist Reconstructionists look askance at the other key draw of evangelical churches and that is the experiential dimension. The Calvinists sing staid songs, read the Bible and weighty theological treatises. What's going on especially in the charismatic churches is something else. There Christians by the thousands are flocking to wild faith healing extravaganzas where people shout and cry and fall on the floor because they are "slain in the spirit." The latest trend is called "holy laughter" whereby the Holy Spirit supposedly leads crowds to roll on the floor laughing uncontrollably, sometimes for hours. This kind of stuff is happening in churches all over the country—often televised for the Christian TV networks—with the backing of prominent evangelical leaders. Some critics have condemned the eccentric antics but they miss the point that people go to church not to read books but to experience something extraordinary. Many get a similar high from joining a political crusade. Large numbers of politically active evangelicals are not going to want to sit still for boring philosophical lectures on how their personal experiences don't matter in the face of pre-ordained reality.

The Founding Fathers Said So

They do sit still, by the thousands, for David Barton of WallBuilders, Inc. From a place called Aledo, Texas, Barton has successfully mass marketed a version of dominion theology that has made his lectures, books and tapes among the hottest properties in the born-again business. With titles like *The Myth of Separation* and *America: to Pray or Not to Pray*, Barton's pitch is that, with the possible exception of Benjamin Franklin, the Founding Fathers were all evangelicals who intended to make this a Christian nation.

Three times last summer I saw crowds of home schoolers and the Christian Coalition go wild with applause for Barton's performance. With an overhead projector, he flashes slides of the Founding Fathers and reels off selected quotes from them saying things like "only the righteous shall rule." Then Barton shifts to a second set of slides. For the years following the Supreme Court's 1962 and 1963 decisions against public school prayer, his charts and graphs show statistical declines in SAT scores and rising rates of teenage promiscuity, drug abuse and other bad behavior. Apparently no one has ever explained to Barton that a mere sequence of unrelated events does not add up to a cause and effect relationship.

Barton's bottom line is that only "the righteous" should occupy public office. This is music to the ears of Christian Right audiences. To grasp Barton's brand of dominion theology, unlike with the Reconstructionists, one does not need a seminary degree. Barton's pseudo-history fills a need most Americans have, to know more about our country's past. His direct linkage of the deified Founding Fathers with contemporary social problems cuts through the evangelicals' theological sectarianism and unites them in a feasible project. They may not be able to take dominion over the whole earth or even agree about when Jesus will return, but they sure can go home and back a godly candidate for city council, or run themselves. Barton tells his audiences that they personally have an important role to play in history, and that is what makes his dominion theology popular.

To Rule and Reign

But Barton's message flies in the face of the Christian Coalition's public claims about wanting only its fair share of political power. In his new book *Politically Incorrect*, Coalition director Ralph Reed writes: "What do religious conservatives really want? They want a place at the table in the conversation we call democracy. Their commitment to pluralism includes a place for faith among the many other competing interests in society." Yet the Coalition's own national convention last September opened with a plenary speech by Rev. D. James Kennedy who echoed the Reconstructionist line when he said that "true Christian citizenship" includes a cultural mandate to "take dominion over all things as vice-regents of God."

Who is telling the truth about the Christian Right's bid for power, Ralph Reed or the popular dominionists who speak at Christian Coalition gatherings? Liberal critics of the Christian Right would have us believe that Reed and Pat Robertson are just plain lying when they say they want to work hand-in-hand, like good pluralists, with non-Christians in government. To bolster the "stealth" thesis, liberals have to resort to conspiracy theory: Barton and Kennedy spoke at the conference, so Reed must secretly agree with them.

A better explanation is that the Christian Right, like other mass movements before it, is a bundle of internal contradictions which work themselves out in the course of real political activism. Ideas have consequences, but it is also true that ideas have causes, rooted in interests and desires. The Christian Right is in a genuine state of tension and flux over its own mission. Part a movement to resist and roll back even moderate change, part just a more reactionary wing of prevailing Republicanism, the Christian Right wants to take dominion and collaborate with the existing political-economic system, both at the same time. Liberal critics, who also endorse the ruling system, can recognize only the Christian Right's takeover dimension. Radicals can see that the dominion project is dangerous because it is, in part, business as usual.

School Days, Rule Days

Z Magazine, October 1994

One of the Christian Right's strengths has been its success in attacking secular institutions while simultaneously building an alternative subculture. Education is a case in point. In a number of school districts, from central Florida to San Diego county, Christian rightists have blocked Head Start programs, sex education and multicultural curricula. But public school battles would be even fiercer were it not for the thousands of evangelical families who have dropped out of the system altogether.

Most, though certainly not all, home schoolers are born-again Christians, and estimates of their numbers range widely. The most recent Department of Education study estimates between 248,500 and 353,500 home schooled students, which is less than one percent of the total school-age population. Michael Farris of the Home School Legal Defense Association claims there are 700,000 to one million home school students. Department of Education researcher Patricia Lines says Farris' figures are high because he includes pre-school aged children and an unknown number of students who, though officially enrolled in private Christian academies, spend part of their school week learning at home. Lines also says Farris' figure reflects the growth of home schooling just in the past few years.

Home schooling is common in rural areas, and it's perfectly legal. Most states require only a high school diploma from parents who teach at home. Existing data show that home schooled students perform better than average on achievement tests in basic subjects. And why wouldn't they? Compared with public school classrooms packed with 30 or more students, proper home schooling gives kids one-to-one training in reading, writing, math, etc.

The drive for higher academic achievement is probably the least salient reason why thousands of Christian parents have dropped out of public schools. For the ranks of the Christian Right, home schooling is more than a private choice. It is a trend with profound political implications. Home schooling is one means through which the Right is solidifying a narrow, reactive ideology among parents and their children.

Home schooling advocates reinforce parents' political justifications for the private choice they've made. For example, in one of the movement's most popular books, *The Right Choice*, Home School Legal Defense Association attorney Christopher Klicka urges Christians to break free from the academic, moral and philosophical crises plaguing the public schools. Academically, Klicka claims that "public school history books are filled with pro-Communist propaganda" and that teachers are no longer teaching phonics. Morally, Klicka points to violence, drug abuse and sexual promiscuity, all supposedly promoted by public school teachers who won't teach real values but do teach kids New Age meditation techniques. Philosophically, Klicka writes, the danger lies in the humanist underpinnings of public education since the 19th century. After all, educational philosopher John Dewey was the first president of the American Humanist Association. "Knowing this," Klicka asks, "can we risk sending our children to public school?" And what may happen as more parents decline such a risk? In the coming years, home school graduates will form the backbone for a new generation of Christian Right activists.

Months after the fact, Christian home school activists are still buzzing about their legislative victory last winter. An amendment attached to a Congressional education bill would have required home school teachers to be state-certified in all subjects they teach. But once the bill was publicized on Christian radio stations, home schoolers flooded Congress with faxes and 800,000 constituent phone calls. The amendment was swiftly removed from the bill, and the home schooling movement had its first taste of nationwide lobbying power.

Politics aside, home schooling also spells big bucks for about a dozen leading producers of curricula materials. I got on the mailing lists of a just a few, and was soon deluged with stacks of catalogs, magazines, and free samples, all with a fundamentalist bent. The largest producer of home school materials is called A-Beka School Services, the publishing arm of Pensacola Christian College in Florida. A-Beka sells textbook and educational video sets for 680,000 students each year. Customers include home schoolers plus 24,000 private schools. A-Beka's catalog begins with the advisory that its editorial department "has rejected the humanistic philosophy and methods of the progressive educators and has turned to original sources and the writings of true scholars. Of course, the most original source is always the Word of God, which is the only foundation for true scholarship in any area of human endeavor." From there, the curriculum for grades K to 12 includes Bible study, history, math, science/health, and language skills. For each subject, A-Beka provides age-appropriate books, flash cards, maps, games and workbooks. The math materials are the most straightforward. I don't know what A-Beka's 11th grade "Christian chemistry text" entails. But the 10th grade biology curriculum is called "God's Living Creation," and A-Beka boasts that it is "truly non-evolutionary in philosophy, spirit, and sequence of study." The reading, history and government materials are the most heavily ideological. No multiculturalism here. The early reading textbooks are all about Jesus, the pilgrims, and other famous white guys. The high-school government text is "written from the standpoint of Biblical Christianity and political and economic conservatism...The concepts of private property, free enterprise, profit and capital, and limited government are clearly presented."

A Real Job

I found more evidence of Christian home schooling's links to right-wing politics at a hot August conference entitled "God, Give Us Men: A Gathering for Home-School Fathers and their Wives." Since I am neither a father nor a wife, I felt just a wee bit out of place at the Zion Fellowship Four-Square Gospel church in Danville, one of the Bay area's wealthiest suburbs. (The Four-Square denomination was founded by Aimee Semple McPherson in 1923.) The 300 some-odd men and their wives—paired off like they were headed for Noah's Ark—assembled at the ungodly hour of 8 a.m. for the latest briefings by a few of the home schooling subculture's leading figures.

Gregg Harris' Christian Life Workshops organizes dozens of similar conferences all over the country. From his home in

Gresham, Oregon, Harris, father of six, is a major distributor of home schooling products in his own right. He spent part of the Saturday conference doing a show-and-tell of new educational products. One was a wall chart to train young children to perform household chores in exchange for paper money, redeemable for toys at the end of each week. Harris was particularly excited about a new board game, "The Richest Christian," a sort of religious version of Monopoly that sells for $23. The goal of the game is for players to "lay up treasures in heaven" by accumulating money that can then be shared charitably with others.

The conferences' main draw, though, was Michael Farris, father of nine and president of the Home School Legal Defense Association. Farris co-founded the HSLDA in 1983, around the same time as he was hired to head the legal department for Concerned Women for America. In the past decade, HSLDA has grown to employ several dozen attorneys, representing some 37,000 member families. For an annual fee of $100, these families rely on HSLDA for legal advice in dealing with local truant officers and school districts. Also in the past decade, home schooling has been recognized as legal in every state, though precise restrictions vary from one place to the next. California's Education Code, for example, requires parents to make attendance records available to school officials and to file an annual private school affidavit with the county superintendent; or to use a public school independent study curriculum; or to enroll as a "satellite program" of an accredited private school. HSLDA helps parents navigate their state's educational codes and represents them in court if need be.

In 1993 Farris made his first bid for public office. He lost his campaign for the lieutenant governorship of Virginia. But he won 46 percent of the vote and is now considered a major power broker in Virginia's Republican Party. It was Farris' supporters who delivered the GOP Senate nomination to Oliver North last spring. Farris has also started a new political action committee, the Madison Project, which will recruit and help bankroll first-time Congressional candidates, not incumbents who already have lists of donors. At the Danville home schooling conference, Farris' Madison Project brochures were stacked high on the entry table, along with a brochure to recruit volunteers for the 1994 reelection campaign of local Congressmember Bill Baker, a darling of the Christian Right. Farris' Saturday morning address was vintage "family values" material. His primary purpose was to instruct fathers on their God-ordained duty to be the spiritual leaders of their families. Farris said that "home schooling is the most effective means of spiritual discipling invented," and he stressed that the real opponent of home schooling is "the enemy of our soul," also known as Satan. To keep the devil at bay, home schooling fathers, not mothers, bear the brunt of the home schooling responsibility. Since dads go to work and moms stay at home, dads have to delegate responsibility to moms. "But when you understand whose job it really is," Farris said, "there's a change in attitude."

Dads should be "deeply grateful" to their wives for performing two full-time jobs, that of homemaker and school teacher. To show their gratitude, husbands should insist that their wives take a daily break—Farris recommended a 30-minute outdoor walk. Husbands should install telephone answering machines so moms won't be pestered by annoying daytime phone calls. Husbands should take wives out to dinner "once in a while," and they should help with the housework. Wow. Farris jokingly clued the audience in on what he calls his "lazy man's" trick: "When you first come home, wash the dishes for the first 30 minutes. Your wife will be so impressed, you can coast for the rest of the night."

Farris continued his litany, all to the effect that moms and dads have rigidly different roles to play in parenting. Moms should be more influential with babies and young kids. Dads are the ones responsible for preparing children for careers, marriage, and political activism. Here things got interesting. Farris explained that children, even teenagers, should not be allowed any boy-girl relationships—not until they are mature enough to consider marriage. To let kids have seemingly cute and harmless friendships with the opposite sex is to encourage teenage sexuality and all the heartbreak that follows. Farris allows no dating, only courtship. Courtship is non-frivolous male-female socializing where the primary goal is to find compatible marriage partners. Courtship must be strictly supervised by both sets of parents and allowed only between fellow believers who are also physically attracted to each other. Farris noted how quickly young men would pass through college or career training programs if they were not allowed to marry (or have sex) until they could support a wife financially.

Everyone in the audience seemed to keep a straight face. We eagerly awaited a break to stretch and go shopping in the church's downstairs exhibit hall. I followed a home schooling father clad in a particularly intriguing T-shirt. The front side said "My wife has a real job," and the back said "...loving me." Downstairs I found the makers of these T-shirts set up in their own booth and wearing the ladies' version. The front says "Get a real job...." The backside reads "...be a wife and mother!" and then lists some of the requisite job skills: arbitrator, nutritionist, chauffeur, nurse, chef, hairdresser, janitor—even lover.

The exhibit hall was filled with a dizzying array of home school product sellers, all doing a brisk business. I looked and fortunately found no materials advocating harsh discipline of children. I found parents loading up on all kinds of books and games for their kids.

One impressive item was a quarterly magazine, *New Attitude*, published by Gregg Harris' son Joshua and a crew of home-schooled teenagers. The magazine is lively and graphically entertaining. It's packed with letters pages, advice columns, features on political campaigns, anti-abortion activism, even a critique of Rush Limbaugh. Editor Joshua Harris, aged 19 and not yet a father, travels around the country preaching teenage sexual abstinence and the virtues of courtship, not dating.

While shopping and snacking on the church lawn, most of the home schoolers seemed to know each other. They'd come from all over northern California. They are well organized, not just in churches, but also through local parents' support groups and the Christian Home Educators' Association, which has chapters in most states.

Stars and Stripes

One of the cornerstones of Christian Right thinking these days is the claim that America's Founding Fathers intended to create a Christian nation. The leading purveyor of this view now is David Barton, who runs a lucrative book and tape sales operation called WallBuilders, Inc. Barton has become ubiquitous on the Christian Right lecture circuit, and he was a featured speaker at the Danville home schooling workshop. I had seen his performance earlier this summer at a meeting of the northern California Christian Coalition. On both occasions I was struck by Barton's popularity with audiences, despite—or maybe because of—his demeanor. Looking like a 30-something cross between Pat Robertson and Ross Perot, Barton wears a big, gawdy stars-and-stripes tie. He never cracks a smile and does not take questions from the floor. He hammers his audiences with a high-speed litany of selected pro-Christian quotes from the leaders of the original thirteen colonies. On an overhead projector, he flashes portraits of the Founders so fast that no one could possibly absorb his "information."

Yet the audiences are riveted by Barton's pitch. With charts and bar graphs, Barton shows a "correlation" between the Supreme Court's 1962 and 1963 decisions removing prayer from public schools and subsequent drastic statistical increases in teenage pregnancies, drug abuse and the like. All of society's problems can be blamed on the fact that Christians did not fight back when the secular humanists pushed God and the Bible out of the public arena. The Founders wanted no such thing as a separation of church and state. On the contrary, Barton selects quotes from people like William Penn to the effect that "only the godly shall rule." For the Christian Coalition meeting, Barton elaborated this point to the effect that *only* Christians should occupy elected offices—and he got a standing ovation.

Barton's pseudo-history and laughable abuse of statistics ought to be an embarrassment to those Christian Right leaders now trying to claim a mainstream mantle. But Barton's popularity should not be dismissed because it points to what motivates much of the movement's following. Here we have a group of people who mix separatism with the belief that Christians—narrowly defined—ought to have dominion over secular society. This is a movement that wants to have its cake and eat it, too.

In *The Right Choice*, Christopher Klicka suggests that conservative Christian parents should stay away from home schoolers of different political and religious persuasions. Yet for the most part, Christian homeschoolers are unwilling to just head for the hills and leave everyone else alone. Some Christian Right activists are fighting to remove liberal educational materials from the public schools while their own kids attend private or home schools. From the safety of their own legally protected churches and private academies, this segment of the Christian Right is training up a new generation to wage what they call "spiritual warfare" all the way into the next millennium.

Focus on Some Families

Z Magazine, July/August 1994

Critics of the Christian Right have seized on the movement's "stealth" tactics to portray a growing number of evangelical activists as "extremists" operating outside the bounds of our supposedly democratic system. It is true that in some parts of the country the Right has taken over school boards and local Republican party central committees by running slates of first-time candidates without publicizing their organizational ties. But this late in the game it is overly simplistic and downright dishonest to blame the Christian Right's continuing local electoral and legislative successes on the work of a handful of covert operators. What accounts for the movement's forward march toward power is its relentless organizing within churches, made possible by the network of Christian broadcast stations, magazines and newspapers, unfettered by the mainstream press. If ever there was a movement that knew how to use alternative media and do grassroots organizing, it is the Christian Right.

And the content of much of this organizing would surprise outsiders. We've become accustomed to thinking that all the Christian Right wants to do is bulldoze its own people into elected office. But reality is more subtle than that, as I learned during a recent all-day Community Impact Seminar, sponsored by the Focus on the Family mega-radio ministry in different cities almost every weekend. This one was held at an Assemblies of God church in Fremont, California, and drew about 200 participants—only about a dozen of whom were ministers—from the Bay area and further south.

One of the first things one needs to take note of at this sort of gathering is the parking lot. There were plenty of late model Hondas and Oldsmobiles with the obligatory fish-shaped ornament on the rear. There was an "I'm the NRA" bumper sticker, but there was also one that said "Don't trust the liberal media," and I wondered where I could get one of those.

The two guys who conducted the seminar did not fit the

stereotype of what they themselves kept jokingly referring to as "right-wing fundamentalist fanatics." From headquarters in Colorado Springs, Focus on the Family sends two alternating teams of intellectuals to present a seven-hour set of polished and compelling motivational lectures. Allen Crippen has a master's degree from Westminster Theological Seminary and used to be a development director for a missionary youth group in Colorado. Greg Jesson is a philosophy professor who got his Ph.D. from the University of Southern California. Jesson was a student of the late philosopher Francis Schaeffer whose 1981 book *A Christian Manifesto* remains one of the most influential treatises on why evangelicals need to be active in politics.

The day began with a session answering the question "Why should Christians be socially and politically involved?" Crippen stressed that fear, anger and hatred are exactly the wrong reasons. Using an overhead slide projector and a litany of Bible verses, Crippen said evangelicals should be active out of "love of neighbor," to more effectively evangelize and save souls, and because Christians are obliged to be good citizens—unless "unjust" laws require them to commit civil disobedience. Crippen and Jesson made frequent references to the immorality of abortion and homosexuality but their purpose was not to fan those flames. "Our desire today is not to whip you up and turn you loose on the Bay area like a bunch of pit bulls," Crippen said. The lesson seemed to be that Christians need affirmative justifications for their activism.

The speakers sought to downplay some of the disreputable misinformation widely circulated within the Christian Right. For example, a number of organizations specialize in selling pseudo-historical books and tapes claiming that America's Founding Fathers were all Bible-believing Christians and that, therefore, this ought to be a "Christian nation." Some of Focus on the Family's own affiliates promote this line. But Crippen tried to clean up the revisionist act a bit by acknowledging that some of the Founding Fathers, e.g., Benjamin Franklin, were not Christians at all. "Be careful," he said. "Precision in this area is essential to advancing the First Amendment debate." Nevertheless, Crippen said, all the Founding Fathers shared a "Christian cultural consensus," and nowhere but in one of Thomas Jefferson's letters to a group of

Baptists did any of the Fathers mention a wall separating church and state.

Greg Jesson extended Crippen's point on the need for more accurate information. He argued that Christians will fail to solve society's "crisis of cultural authority" if they follow the strategy of others on the Christian Right who think the answer is to replace the "gatekeepers"—elites in government, media, education, law and entertainment—with people who claim to be born-again. (Interestingly, he omitted corporate elites, many of whom are already mainstays of right-wing support.) Jesson cited survey data culled by Christian pollster George Barna, showing that 66 percent of the public—including a large percentage of self-identified evangelicals—does not believe in such a thing as "absolute truth." Jesson told the activists that they are "in danger of a massive misdiagnosis of culture" if they proceed as if there really is a "moral majority" in America. Recognizing that Bible-believing Christians represent only a minority of Americans, he urged the activists to stop condemning their political opponents and to start learning to speak persuasively to a "post-Christian culture."

Jesson traced the roots of Christianity's declining influence to shifts in Western culture's dominant philosophical paradigm over the past few hundred years: from reliance on Aristotelian and Christian thought to scientific empiricism and from there downward to relativism and subjectivism. I agreed with Jesson's claim that relativism and subjectivism leave one able to truly "know" only one's own group or one's personal feelings. But he blamed subjectivism and its resulting nihilism on science— because scientists have different vantage points—which was a great leap of logic. In any event, it was the kind of lecture one would expect to hear in a university hall but not on the floor of a pentecostal church.

Capital and Resources

The Community Impact Seminar's highbrow approach was not altogether surprising. It seems obvious that Focus on the Family wants to weed out the rubes and flakes who just want to get political without any forethought. Those not turned-off by the first seminar's lofty content can sign up for subsequent trainings and political campaign schools where the substance is more practical. Beyond this natural selection process, though, Focus' toned down rhetoric seems intended as a corrective to some of the Christian Right's recent excesses. Violence at abortion clinics, cruel anti-gay rhetoric and the stealth election tactics of partisan groups like the Christian Coalition have not only outraged the general public. Such antics have also kept some of the Christian Right's own would-be constituents reluctant to get involved. The Community Impact Seminar is designed to break through this impasse by training already seasoned activists to motivate uninvolved members of their own churches. Theoretically, each person who attends the seminar is supposed to go back to his or her church and start a committee that will keep the whole church informed and ready to spring into action with legislative lobbying, boycotts, clinic blockades and the like.

Focus on the Family started conducting these seminars about three years ago, in conjunction with a network of affiliated state think tanks now numbering three dozen. In California, the Sacramento-based Capitol Resource Institute (CRI) tracks legislation and mobilizes grassroots lobbyists via Christian broadcast stations and about 100 "community impact committees" up and down the state.

CRI is a perfect example of how large infusions of capital from a few rich donors, combined with pressure in the name of large numbers of constituents give the Christian Right the capacity to wield clout within state legislatures. CRI is funded largely by the California Christian Right's two major benefactors, Howard Ahmanson and Robert Hurtt. Ahmanson is the heir to the Home Savings of America dynasty. Hurtt owns a lucrative container supply company. In 1988, Ahmanson, Hurtt and two other Christian business leaders formed the Capitol Commonwealth Group, through which they have spent over a million dollars electing new right-wing members of the California state legislature. In 1993, Hurtt got himself elected to the state Senate.

But Hurtt is only one of what CRI calls its "family-friendly legislators." According to the think tank's monthly newsletter, at the start of the 1994 legislative session, CRI hosted a breakfast for 17 friendly members of the California Assembly and Senate who "affirmed their commitment to traditional family values" and began receiving CRI's twice weekly "Blue Page" sheet recommending "yes" or "no" votes on each piece of family-related legislation. State Senator Tim Leslie helped CRI establish the group of pro-Christian Right legislators, who call themselves the Conference on the Preservation of the Family. These elected officials understand the power of the Ahmanson-Hurtt consortium to make or break elections, and they also understand the kind of grassroots muscle CRI can marshal, at will. Among this year's priorities, CRI has organized a group of medical doctors, the California Physicians Advisory Council, which is currently sponsoring two state bills that, if passed, would require county health officials to identify HIV positive individuals. (The bills' sponsors are the same people who want to ban laws protecting gays and lesbians from housing and employment discrimination.)

On the education front, CRI has been a leader in the fight to remove supposedly invasive and "anti-family" skills testing from the California Learning Assessment System (CLAS) exam administered to public elementary and high school students. This public brouhaha began in late 1993. Under pressure from Louis Sheldon's Traditional Values Coalition, California's Department of Education removed from this year's tenth grade CLAS test Alice Walker's short story "Roselily," on grounds that the story was "anti-religious." Amid public controversy the Board of Education voted to restore "Roselily." But by then a slew of Christian Right groups realized the hay they could make with the CLAS test.

The prelude to this spring's campaign against CLAS was a surprise victory for the Christian Right on a failed Congressional bill to regulate home schooling teachers. In February Congressmember George Miller (D-CA) added to a House education bill an amendment that would have required private and home school teachers to be state-certified in all subjects they teach. About a week before the scheduled vote, attorney Michael Farris, president of the 37,000-member Home School Legal Defense Association, leapt into action. Through interviews on Christian radio stations and through a fax and phone tree network of home schoolers' associations in every state, Farris and others mobilized an estimated 800,000 constituent calls to

Congress against H.R. 6. Reportedly, in one week there were more calls to Congress over this bill than there were against gays in the military, and in the end, every member of Congress except George Miller voted against state certification of home school teachers. Farris attributed the victory in large part to his appearances on Marlin Maddoux's U.S.A. Radio Network and Dr. James Dobson's Focus on the Family radio show, both nationally syndicated.

On the heels of the H.R. 6 victory, CRI and various Christian Right radio hosts kept the school issue fires burning. In California, they turned toward the CLAS test, and people who admitted they have never even seen the test began circulating apocryphal stories about its contents. One widely repeated story claims that the math portion of the test includes a word problem asking students how they would divide 17 apples between four students. If the test were really about measuring math skills, they say, the answer would be to give each student four and a quarter apples. But CLAS opponents say the only "politically correct" answer is to divide sixteen apples evenly and then give the remaining one to the student who is most needy. That, they say, is socialist brainwashing!

CLAS was developed several years ago as an alternative to multiple choice achievement tests. CLAS requires students to explain their math answers, perform thought experiments, and demonstrate their reading comprehension by writing essay answers and relating what they read to their own experiences. The idea of more than one "correct" answer has driven educational reactionaries up the wall. They see CLAS as part of a broader conspiracy by educational elites to impose Outcome Based Education (OBE), an umbrella term used to describe state and local curricular initiatives that, if implemented, would work on students' "self-esteem" and require them to demonstrate problem-solving skills beyond the three R's.

Amid the flurry of propaganda aimed at CLAS and OBE, the Rutherford Institute, a Christian Right legal firm, in April sued the California Department of Education to stop school districts from administering the CLAS test without parental consent. Rutherford also sued individual school districts and, in several counties, won temporary restraining orders for parents who want their children exempted from the CLAS test altogether. At this writing, and only a few weeks into the anti-CLAS campaign, California Governor Pete Wilson has ordered an audit of the CLAS test, and the state schools superintendent has proposed making portions of the test public to alleviate parental fears.

In essence, the Christian Right has found in the CLAS test an ideal activist campaign with virtually no down sides. Either the movement succeeds in getting the test removed, modified or defunded, or rightists will enjoy a permanent pseudo-atrocity they can point to in their claims that the state is undermining "family values." Among the very few printed materials available at the Focus on the Family Community Impact Seminar was the Capitol Resource Institute's packet on how to lobby state legislators against CLAS.

In Focus

Focus on the Family, like many other evangelical organizations, is both a religious ministry and a political project. At the helm of the $90 million a year operation is psychologist Dr. James Dobson, whose best-selling book on child-rearing *Dare to Discipline* has made him a kind of born-again Dr. Spock. Dobson's popularity has grown steadily since he founded Focus in 1977. Presently, Dobson's half-hour daily radio broadcast airs on 1,400 mostly Christian stations, and every month Dobson's staff answers about 250,000 letters from listeners seeking marital, family and personal advice. On the air, Dobson, the homespun radio persona hosts guests on predictable "family" themes. Recent program titles have included: "Facing Your Financial Future," "Hope for the Homosexual," "Positive Parenting," and "Group Pressure and How to Handle It." Off-air, more than two million people receive Focus' ten different magazines. There is one for radio listeners, two for young children, three for teenagers, one each for parents, teachers and physicians.

There is also a monthly magazine for political activists. *Citizen* magazine has 200,000 subscribers who also receive a free monthly newsletter from the Family Research Council (FRC). In 1988 Dobson joined forces with this Washington, D.C,. think tank, headed by former Reagan aide Gary Bauer. Focus and FRC recently cut their legal ties so that Bauer's staff can do full-fledged lobbying without jeopardizing Focus' educational tax status.

But contrary to its projected image as just another evangelical ministry, Focus is overtly partisan. In 1992 Dobson and company played pivotal roles in the passage of Colorado's anti-gay rights Amendment 2. As the Amendment's sponsors Colorado for Family Values tell it in their new book *Gay Politics vs. Colorado and America*, the petition drive to put the initiative on the ballot was floundering until Dr. Dobson decided to air a nationwide radio program about it. Suddenly, recalls CFV's Kevin Tebedo, "Our phones began ringing off the wall. We had volunteers suddenly begging to carry petitions." And according to a recent exposé of CFV's tactics by *S.F. Bay Times* reporter Tim Kingston, Focus helped CFV by producing public service announcements aired on nearly every radio station in Colorado.

Nor was the Colorado campaign an isolated foray into electoral politics. In issue after issue of the *Citizen* magazine, Focus trumpets its latest contributions to the Christian Right's agenda. Through its three dozen family policy councils, and in coordination with Christian radio stations, Focus produces 60-second announcements for local activist groups. In 1990 in Washington state, Focus aired spots to recruit petition gatherers for an anti-abortion state ballot initiative. In Ohio Focus aired spots to calls to legislators to protest a sex education program.

Focus has been particularly active on the anti-gay rights front. In 1989 Dobson took credit for using radio broadcasts and personal letters to pastors to bring out the vote against gay rights measures in three California cities. Last year, in Lewiston, Maine, Focus helped an inexperienced couple establish a committee that succeeded in repealing a local gay rights ordinance.

The Power and the Glory

Wherever the action is, Focus on the Family moves to the front of the parade. Dobson has consistently endorsed Operation Rescue and recently played a key role in founding the Alliance Defense Fund, which will coordinate fundraising for a half dozen Christian Right legal firms.

On any given issue there is tremendous synergy between what happens over the airwaves, in the courtrooms and in churches behind the scenes. While Pat Robertson dominates the Christian television medium, James Dobson is the movement's single most influential radio personality. Robertson's Christian Coalition is now an undisguised faction of the Republican party. Dobson's Focus on the Family combines activist training with more subtle cultural programming aimed at a potentially broader audience. Deliberately or not, the movement has developed a division of labor that allows activists of different dispositions to do what they can do best. Some will keep challenging the existing power structure by running for elected office. Others are quietly building parallel institutions in law, education and media. One does not have to agree with the Christian Right's policy agenda to see that this is good, common sense organizing.

See Them in Court

Z Magazine, April 1994

Two recent trends signal the Christian Right's capacity to make the kind of strategic shifts successful movements must make. Overtures to recruit clergy of color, combined with recent public relations efforts to soften the movement's rhetorical pitch, are both responses to critics' charges of racism and "extremism." Another sign of the Christian Right's growing maturity has been the proliferation of legal firms prepared to take evangelicals' political battles to court.

A case that began in San Francisco last summer has raised the public profile of the Rutherford Institute, until recently the Christian Right's preeminent law firm. The Rutherford Institute is now suing San Francisco Mayor Frank Jordan for alleged "religious discrimination" in the removal, last year, of Rev. Eugene Lumpkin from the city's Human Rights Commission. Rev. Lumpkin, an African-American Baptist minister, had inflamed public sentiment with his repeated claims about the "abomination" of homosexuality. One thing led to another. The San Francisco board of supervisors voted to remove Lumpkin from the commission. The Bay area outpost of Lou Sheldon's Traditional Values Coalition then rallied behind Lumpkin. The impolitic preacher told a local TV talk show host that he concurred with the Old Testament prescription of stoning "sodomites" to death. Under political pressure, Jordan fired Lumpkin.

The Rutherford Institute volunteered to represent Lumpkin free of charge in a suit against the mayor. Rutherford's western regional director Brad Dacus sees the pending case as a potential precedent-setter: can a city fire someone, even from a sensitive human rights post, on the basis of "a theological answer to a theological question?" If the answer is "yes," Dacus says, Christians will be subject to a form of "religious gerrymandering" that could rule out their serving on school boards, city councils and the like.

This is exactly the kind of legal conflict that conservative

Christians will inevitably land in as they carry their sectarian religious views into supposedly democratic institutions. Cases like Lumpkin's have fueled the growth of half a dozen different Christian legal firms in recent years. At the February 1994 convention of the National Religious Broadcasters in Washington, D.C., Christian Right leaders announced a new Alliance Defense Fund, which plans to eventually raise and channel $25 million annually to fight anti-abortion, pro-school prayer and "religious liberty" cases in court.

Lawyers, Guns, and Money

Already the most visible of the Christian Right firms has scored some major victories. The American Center for Law and Justice, founded in 1991 and based at Pat Robertson's Virginia Beach headquarters, won the 1993 Supreme Court ruling that abortion clinic blockades are not a violation of women's civil rights. Another Supreme Court ruling upheld church groups' "equal access" to after-school campus facilities. In a lower federal court case, ACLJ won a ruling allowing student-led prayers at high school graduations. ACLJ's chief litigator Jay Sekulow specializes in big, splashy cases. In ACLJ's promotional literature, Sekulow boasts that he's got "a SWAT team of freedom fighters; poised and eager to defend these rights in state and federal courts, and even at meetings of local school boards and city councils."

Before joining Robertson in Virginia Beach, Sekulow ran an Atlanta-based ministry, Christian Advocates Serving Evangelism (CASE), and made frequent promotional appearances on Trinity Broadcasting Network's "Praise the Lord" talk show. Press profiles never fail to mention that Sekulow is a Brooklyn-born Jewish convert who cut his legal teeth defending—before the Supreme Court—the rights of Jews for Jesus to proselytize in airports.

Sekulow and the ACLJ say they accept no fees for legal services. But the firm has a built-in donor base, courtesy of Pat Robertson's lucrative Christian Coalition and Christian Broadcasting Network mailing lists. Now Sekulow appears regularly on Robertson's "700 Club" show, and he has his own show on the Trinity Broadcasting Network.

Dramatic cases and loads of media attention have helped

ACLJ steal the thunder from the more modest Rutherford Institute. Started by attorney John Whitehead in 1982, Rutherford has until recently been the pioneer of Christian legal firms, specializing in the defense of anti-abortion protesters and "parents' rights" to home school their children. From its five regional offices, every month Rutherford issues a slew of press releases on its cases, some petty, others weighty. Here are a few recent examples:

- An appeal by a Wisconsin woman who was fined $8,000 after she ran an allegedly discriminatory housing ad for a "Christian handyman."

- A judgment that a Mississippi nursing home employee, fired for refusing to hang Halloween decorations, cannot be denied state unemployment benefits.

- A suit against a Texas junior college by a student who was told to stop distributing religious tracts on campus.

- Another suit against a Denver shopping center for ordering two teenage "Warriors for Christ" evangelists to leave the mall.

Consistently, Rutherford takes cases that would strengthen the public role of conservative Christians, though occasionally on civil liberties principles that cut across the political spectrum. Months before the persecution of Chamula Indians in Chiapas, Mexico, made national headlines, for example, the Rutherford Institute's Latin American branch petitioned the Mexican government to redress land seizures and other violations of indigenous Protestants' rights by the dominant Catholic church. Here at home, though, during the public battle over gay military personnel, the Rutherford Institute claimed that lifting the ban would threaten religious liberty, unless the military moved "to exempt religious people from compelled personal acceptance of homosexuality." In a recent Rutherford magazine interview, founding attorney John Whitehead said the most controversial case he's ever handled was defending Operation Rescue clinic blockaders who—contrary to stereotype—were not overwhelmingly endorsed even by fellow anti-abortionists. "People withdrew financial support; in one year alone we lost over $100,000 in contributions. We stuck to our guns and did it anyway," Whitehead said.

With an annual budget of $11 million (about twice that of the ACLJ) and nine staff attorneys, Rutherford claims to do 80 percent of the total case work in the fields of religious discrimination, defense of anti-abortion protesters, and "parents' rights." Several small firms pick up much of the slack. The Christian Legal Society, founded in 1975, files friend-of-the-court briefs for individual Christian attorneys and helps mediate out-of-court disputes between evangelical leaders and churches. The Home School Legal Defense Association, headed by Michael Farris (who in 1993 ran unsuccessfully for Virginia's lieutenant governorship), provides specialized counsel and channels inquiring parents into state-based Christian home schooling associations.

The Western Center for Law and Religious Freedom, with offices in Washington, Oregon, and California, takes on local cases similar to those handled by the Rutherford Institute. The Western Center distributes a handy one-page sheet, "Political Guidelines for Pastors and Churches," advising activist churches on how to operate within the boundaries of their IRS tax-exempt status. "Non-partisan" voter registration tables inside the church are fine. But overt electioneering and legislative lobbying may not constitute more than five percent of churches' activity. They can circulate candidates' voting records so long as printed materials include neither endorsements nor editorial comment. Churches may *rent* but not *donate* their mailing lists to specific candidates.

Casting Stones

As the field expands, ACLJ has upstaged other firms, and rivalries have surfaced. Rarely do Christian Right organizations attack each other in print. But in Rutherford's January 1994 magazine issue, legal coordinator Alexis Crow vented her resentment toward ACLJ and made hints about financial improprieties at Robertson's headquarters. "Because the Rutherford Institute has no other agenda and does not raise funds for other programs, it is able to put all of its money into its work; TRI does not build lavish buildings or own for-profit subsidiaries," Crow wrote. "In light of the recent scandals involving religious leaders, people are rightfully suspicious of non-profit groups."

To drive home this point, Rutherford is circulating a lengthy accountability checklist called "Evaluation Guide for Religious Defense Organizations," which asks Christian donors to compare Rutherford's answers with those of other law firms soliciting money. Here are some of the provocative questions intended to distinguish Rutherford from the ACLJ: "Does the organization take cases even where there is no 'precedent' or media value?" "Does the organization have and train more than one 'star' litigator?" "Does the organization use the cases and/or work of other organizations to raise its funds?" The questionnaire ends with an advisory: "The answers to many of these questions will inform you as to why The Rutherford Institute is not affiliated with and has not merged with other organizations involved in the area of religious liberty."

That's a reference to Rutherford's decision not to participate in the new Alliance Defense Fund, a scheme through which Christian Right leaders will selectively fund "religious liberty" and "family preservation" lawsuits in years to come. The ADF represents a serious escalation in the Christian Right's legal action project. The ADF plans to raise $1 million this year, $6 million in 1994. Eventually the plan is to accumulate an endowment that can generate $25 million a year for legal work.

To accomplish this, ADF has brought together some of the movement's biggest guns, including Focus on the Family President Dr. James Dobson, Bill Bright of Campus Crusade for Christ, Gary Bauer of Family Research Council, Donald Wildmon of the American Family Association, Christian financial advisor Larry Burkett, talk show host and USA Radio Network executive Marlin Maddoux, and D. James Kennedy of Coral Ridge Ministries. Joining these heavy hitters, the new ADF board of directors includes National Religious Broadcasters President Dr. E. Brandt Gustavson, former Congressmember Mark Siljander, Bill Bright's businessman friend William Pew, and additional leaders of Campus Crusade and Focus on the Family.

Overseeing the whole operation from ADF's Phoenix headquarters is Alan Sears, a former federal prosecutor who, under the Reagan administration, directed the Attorney General's

Commission on Pornography. More recently Sears directed the National Family Legal Foundation, a Christian law firm specializing in obscenity cases. Sears was tightlipped about ADF's precise sources of funding. But he did tell me he plans to aggressively promote ADF on Christian TV and radio stations.

No longer will individual law firms prioritize their case loads on an ad hoc basis. ADF will review grant proposals and selectively fund and match clients with Christian attorneys. Sears says ADF's client-driven plan will encourage litigation by aggrieved Christians and attorneys not already affiliated with the existing firms, thereby expanding the total amount of legal action. Some of the established firms, though, may stand to benefit from ADF's war chest. The Christian Legal Society has two representatives on ADF's board, and ACLJ media director Gene Kapp says ACLJ's Jay Sekulow has offered to advise ADF.

Thus far, only the Rutherford Institute—which has no representation within ADF—objects to the new project. Rutherford's western regional coordinator Brad Dacus says ADF's grantmaking review board will create an unnecessary and expensive bureaucracy with no sure way for donors to know how their money is spent.

Trials and Tribulations

Who knows if the Christian Right's legal beagles enjoy a subtle irony their professional activism carries? Historically, Christian fundamentalists—and, by extension, other evangelicals—became national laughing stocks in the 1920s when the state of Tennessee put public school teacher John Scopes on trial for teaching evolution. The infamous "monkey trial" humiliated Bible thumpers into retreat from secular institutions. Only decades later would the political mobilization of evangelicals land many of them in legal trouble of one sort or another.

Now the venerable halls of justice offer Christian rightists some limited opportunities to defend—if not further promote—their participation in public affairs. "Religious discrimination" is the battle cry of Christian Right litigants claiming victimization by a society they see as sinful and contemptuous of their faith. Like it or not, evangelical Christians are citizens, too, and they are entitled to legal protection when and if their rights are trampled on. Anti-abortion demonstrators—though many are not as peace-loving as they profess—ought to have the right to assemble and protest. But the Supreme Court now dominated by Reagan and Bush appointees recently ruled that the National Organization for Women can sue abortion protesters as if they were criminal racketeers. How long before the tables are turned and the Christian Right uses conspiracy laws to sue activists on our side of the line?

At one level, the Rutherford Institute's pending case against the mayor of San Francisco may signal how well the Christian Right can use expensive lawsuits to enforce tolerance of its views on board government commissions. At another level, cases like Rev. Eugene Lumpkin's are in court, in the first place, because blatant homophobia no longer goes unchallenged. The Christian Right is building a legal Goliath to fight some battles it knows it may lose.

The Christian Right's Anti-Gay Agenda

The Humanist, July/August 1994

This year's slate of "no special rights" ballot initiatives is the most visible part of the Christian Right's "family values" agenda. In Arizona, Idaho, Michigan, Missouri, Nevada, Oregon, Washington, and Texas, the movement hopes to place on ballots a fairly uniform set of statutes and constitutional amendments that would reverse and pre-empt any laws extending anti-discrimination protections and domestic partners' benefits to gays and lesbians. Already such ballot measures have met with mixed success. Colorado's narrowly passed Amendment 2 was overruled as unconstitutional. The Oregon Citizens' Alliance has won passage of anti-gay ordinances in numerous small counties but not statewide.

Still, there is a method to the apparent madness of the Christian Right's ballot campaigns. Successful or not, they keep gay rights advocates on the defensive. The organized Right—aroused by fear and loathing of homosexuals—can reap the advantages of low voter turn-out, predictable during the mid-term election season. We can expect to see more Christian Right candidates win elected offices, from which they will, in turn, encroach further on secular, civil liberties.

At one level, then, the anti-gay rights campaign is a ploy by political professionals. But there's more to the story. Survey data culled by the National Gay and Lesbian Task Force shows the U.S. public to be divided on the necessity of protective legal measures for gays and lesbians. About three-quarters of the public opposes discrimination on the basis of sexual orientation. But half to three-quarters of the public also think homosexuality is immoral and unacceptable. That means a sizeable segment of the population is receptive to anti-gay rights appeals and, more broadly, to the Christian Right's growing arsenal of homophobic propaganda.

This year, hundreds of thousands of people will vote to deny civil rights to gays and lesbians—not just because they get a flyer from Lou Sheldon or Pat Robertson, but because their worst fears about sexual "deviants" have been stirred up by a virulent and growing cottage industry of anti-gay books, newsletters and videotapes.

The best known of the anti-gay productions is a series of home videos—the prototype was "The Gay Agenda"—produced largely with risqué film footage taken at gay rights marches in San Francisco and Washington, D.C. But the range is much broader, and some of the propaganda themes are particularly ominous. Some of the material is aimed at presenting gays and lesbians as diseased "victims" ripe for healing by Christian counselors. Other materials portray homosexuals as the lynchpins of a sinister conspiracy to destroy American democracy.

To understand—and defeat—the Christian Right's anti-gay rights agenda at the polls, we must delve into the propaganda environment that now invests "queers" with the stigmatized status once reserved for "communists," and now increasingly assigned to Jews and other "foreigners" in Europe's fascist climate.

At the most clinical, but insidious, end of the propaganda spectrum is the California-based Exodus International and its network of some 95 "ex-gay" affiliate ministries around the country. Exodus' goal is to convince gays and lesbians that they can reverse their sexual orientation through prayer and sheer acceptance of Christian mandates against sexual "sin." There is no telling how many real live gays and lesbians take advantage of Exodus' referral service and submit themselves to counselling by lay ministers who have themselves "overcome a homosexual past." Much of Exodus' counselling is geared toward the bereaved parents of adult children hopelessly lost to the "homosexual lifestyle."

Exodus has been around since 1976 but its profile has risen noticeably just in the past few years. Typically, articles in the Christian Right press about AIDS, about politically active gays and lesbians—about anything connected to the "homosexual agenda"—are accompanied by referrals to Exodus and its mail order "Christian General Store" of anti-gay books and tapes. Among the most widely circulated is Joe Dallas' *Desires in Conflict: Answering the Struggle for Sexual Identity.* The book is for Christians struggling to reverse—or repress?—their homosexual tendencies. (This is a dubious pursuit, though certainly some people can and want to change their sexual orientation over time.) The book's tone is conversational and encouraging, but unyielding on the message that gays must "turn or burn." But apart from however many souls Exodus ministries might save, its broader function is less therapeutic than propagandistic. "Former" homosexuals affiliated with Exodus make frequent appearances on Christian TV and radio programs, where their testimonies reinforce the idea—for mostly straight audiences— that homosexuality is demonically inspired.

Some of Exodus' affiliates recently told their stories in a magazine cover story for the mega-radio ministry Focus on the Family. The theme of these stories was the amazing grace that has led ex-gays and lesbians to the heterosexual bliss now so evident in photos of their smiling faces.

The evangelical media's constant repetition of such personal salvation stories is not as innocuous as it might seem. Through its daily broadcasts on more than 1,400 radio stations, its network of several dozen state-based think tanks, and its monthly political magazine *The Citizen,* Focus on the Family has played a large role in mobilizing voters for anti-gay ballot measures nationwide. It is important for Christian Right supporters to believe that gays and lesbians could straighten themselves out just as easily as they might dye their hair pink. By believing that homosexuality is a willfully *chosen* "lifestyle," Christian moralists can more righteously *choose* to deny civil rights to the incorrigible.

The sugar-coated changeability theme seems to work well for the kind of mass homophobic audiences tuned into James Dobson's Focus on the Family. The more committed anti-gay activists seem to need more hard-core stimulation, though, and there is plenty to go around. On the heels of their successful fight against open inclusion of gay military personnel, the producers of the blockbuster "Gay Agenda" video have stayed in business with a new magazine, the *Lambda Report.* Ty and Jeannett Beeson, two nobodys from the Springs of Life church in Lancaster, California, teamed up with writer Peter LaBarbera, a former editor of Concerned Women for America's monthly magazine. LaBarbera writes all the articles, and the Beesons sell subscriptions to the *Lambda Report* for $29.95. Each issue features a story of a gay man or lesbian gone straight. Mostly, though, the magazine reports on grassroots campaigns to head off local gay rights ordinances and harps on two themes central to homophobic propaganda: 1) the pedophilic North American Man Boy Love Association (NAMBLA) as the vanguard of the gay rights movement and 2) wealthy gay rights activists wielding growing—and disproportionate—power over government agencies and politicians.

Together, the package of propaganda themes in the *Lambda Report* is a coherent one: some homosexuals have the decency to repent and change their ways, but most won't because they're perverts who want to infiltrate the Boy Scouts and spend a fortune on the president's inaugural ball and obscene parades in big cities.

The pedophilia theme is vile and crude, pandering to homophobes' dual sense of repulsion and fascination with homosexual fantasies. The excessive power theme follows from Clinton's early moves to reverse the ban on gays-in-the-military, but its psychopolitical value is more expansive. Psychologically speaking, this propaganda allows the Christian Right to project its own power-wielding status onto its enemy-victims. The trick is to divert attention away from the Right's grip on the Republican Party through stories of politicians beholden to the "gay agenda." The *Lambda Report* has focused on Massachusetts Governor William Weld, a liberal Republican, who backed a bill to protect gay students from harassment in public schools. Weld is exceptional among Republicans. But for homophobic propagandists, his stance becomes emblematic.

The political power theme, gone wild, underlies some of the most paranoid, recent additions to the Christian Right's homophobia arsenal. Here we enter the realm of apocalyptic fiction, though fiction peddled in concert with purportedly factual reporting.

During the months when Colorado's Amendment 2 underwent judicial review, its sponsor Colorado for Family Values added to its monthly newsletter serialized excerpts from a forthcoming novel, *Colorado 1988*, in which homosexuals control the government and exact revenge against Bible-believing Christians. In one of the novel's excerpted vignettes, four-year-old Heather is taken from her family and placed in foster care after her teachers identify her as a problem child "being home schooled in a right-wing homophobic home." When Heather's mother refuses to comply with a Family Court order to undergo a Queer Sensitivity Services training session, the child is told she will never see her parents again.

I heard a variation on this theme at the top of a recent pair of anti-gay radio broadcasts aired by Beverly La Haye's Concerned Women for America (estimated audience: 500,000). Each show began with a dramatized interchange between two Christians lamenting, sometime in the near future, that since passage of a federal gay rights bill, all churches have to hire homosexuals—or else be shut down.

At a recent Washington, D.C. meeting of the Traditional Values Coalition, one of the scheduled speakers was author Spenser Hughes, whose novel *The Lambda Conspiracy* takes the cake for the most delusional item in the futuristic horror-fiction genre. I don't want to give away the plot. But after reading the first fifty pages, I could not put the book down—not until I knew if the cabal of gay male New Agers controlling the White House and responsible for killing a Christian U.S. Senator at the evangelical broadcasters' convention would prevail against the handsome, 35-year-old TV journalist who sacrifices fame, fortune and even his fiancée's unborn child to tell the truth about Them, the queers. I don't know if this potboiler is more dangerous because it's published by the reputable Moody Press and widely available in Christian book stores, or because the Traditional Values Coalition is selling the book and promoting author Spenser Hughes as an "information" source fit to share the podium with elected officials and former Secretary of Education William Bennett.

While I could not put *The Lambda Conspiracy* down, neither could I stop thinking, page after page, of Hannah Arendt's explanations of racial bigotry and anti-Semitism in her classic *The Origins of Totalitarianism*. What made Jews the officially designated enemy of Christian Europe was the flip side of the color-based biological determinism that allowed white colonizers to look *downward* and justify their theft of dark-skinned people's resources. With anti-Semitism, the prejudiced mind looks *upward* and sees the mirage of an elite, conspiratorial clique controlling the media, the labor unions, the schools, the government itself. This cabal—the term comes from "Kabbalah," the Hebrew word for mysticism—can become the imagined culprit for large numbers of people who know their society is sick but don't know quite why.

For the mass-based, anti-elite and rhetorically populist Christian Right, gays and lesbians are perfect foils. There aren't very many of Them, but it seems like They are everywhere. They do bad things in the dark, and yet They have the audacity to demand equal rights at a time when everyone knows there is just not enough to go around.

The Christian Right may win some and lose some of its anti-gay rights measures this fall. But the continuing value of picking on a fear-inspiring target is a sure bet.

How Radical is the Christian Right?

The Humanist, March/April 1994

Going on two years after Patrick Buchanan delivered his infamous "cultural warfare" speech at the 1992 GOP convention, I am still invariably asked on radio talk shows: hasn't the Christian Right's "extremism" become a liability for "mainstream" Republicans? My answer, also invariably, is both "yes" and "no."

The Christian Right's flamboyant convention antics scared a lot of television viewers but at the same time signified the movement's arrival as the Republicans' biggest and most reliable constituency. Now as the Christian Right marches steadily, though less noisily, toward assuming political power, movement leaders are themselves debating their future—as unyielding moral crusaders, as rank-and-file Republicans, or as some combination of both these tendencies.

While the Christian Right stands to mature in the process of charting its own course, critics of the movement seem caught with a set of blinders that continue to frame politically active evangelicals as "extremists," somehow coming from outside of and not belonging to "mainstream" culture let alone everyday party politics. But opponents of the Christian Right stand to lose if they fail to recognize that while the movement, indeed, has some wild policy goals, the agenda is supported by millions of people as common as the neighbors next door.

Take last fall's elections in the state of Virginia. The Democrats tried to turn the election into a referendum against Christian Right-backed candidates, and that strategy failed. First-time candidate Michael Farris, a home schooling activist and former attorney for Concerned Women of America, was pilloried as a raving "extremist," lost the race for lieutenant governor but still managed to raise $1 million and win 46 percent of the vote. On the other hand, Governor George F. Allen and Attorney General

James S. Gilmore III, both moderate Republicans, won largely because of support from right-wing evangelicals. (After the election, Allen appointed prominent anti-abortion activists to his transition team and sought to nominate Family Research Council v.p. Kay Cole James as Virginia's secretary of health.) In fact, Democratic gubernatorial candidate Mary Sue Terry saw her poll ratings plummet following negative TV ads and speeches portraying Allen as a darling of Christian Right "extremists." In a state where a third of the voters identify themselves as evangelical Christians, the Democrats' name calling smacked of religious bigotry. Post-election commentators drew the lesson that for mainstream Republicans, Christian Right backing helps more than it hurts.

That's because negative campaigning has limited appeal and because—like it or not—the Christian Right genuinely represents a solid minority of Americans. In some parts of the country, that minority is a majority. Last summer, six Oregon counties passed preemptive measures banning civil rights protections for gay citizens. The measures were sponsored by the activist Oregon Citizens' Alliance, but they won because thousands of voters share the Christian Right's homophobia. To call them all "extremists" will not change the vote tallies.

Why, then, do liberal critics of the Christian Right persistently resort to broad-brush slogans like "extremism" and a related epithet, the "radical right?" I can offer a few reasons. These terms were first popularized during the 1950s and 1960s when prominent political scientists, in dutiful service to the liberal wing of the Cold War establishment, labeled Senator Joseph McCarthy and his admirers as paranoid "radicals," alien to the American body politic. In reality, McCarthy drew his support from the same Republican faithfuls who had elected President Eisenhower. Popular right-wing groups like the John Birch Society emerged only in the late 1950s, well after political elites had turned the pursuit of "communist subversion" into a national religion. By then, polite society was keen to depict wild-eyed Birchers as "extremists," even as they played by democratic rules and helped win the Republican nomination for Barry Goldwater.

Academia's warnings about "radical right extremism" held

influence when the massive Christian Right mobilized in the late 1970s. Throughout the 1980s and continuing now, liberal outfits like People for the American Way have promoted a view of dangerous "radical right" Christians as something separate from the U.S. political-economic system itself. There is nothing particularly "radical" about most politically active evangelical Christians. To be "radical" means to seize the roots of social problems, to advocate and work for profound change. The Christian Right, on the contrary, supports existing conditions that effectively maintain inequality between rich and poor, white and black, men and women. More directly, the Christian Right of the 1980s enlisted in a full gamut of U.S. military operations abroad and now in the 1990s is working to forestall gay civil rights and provisions for accessible abortion within the Clinton health care plan.

Still, liberals organized against the Christian Right can make hay by exploiting the "radical right" paradigm. While performing the valuable service of monitoring electoral races, People for the American Way, for example, needs to ensure its own financial resources and prominence in the media limelight. It can do so most efficiently by projecting its spokespeople as legitimate democratic players battling Christian "extremists" and by sticking to simplistic formulas that avoid controversy. Were liberal critics to analyze the Christian Right as a natural ally of corporate Republicanism, they might find themselves labeled as "radicals." The *New York Times* and CNN would stop calling, and the foundation dollars would dry up.

Then again, the Christian Right's own avowed strategy—until recently—has fed right into the hands of liberals looking to find "extremists." The idea of secretly running Christian Right-backed candidate slates to take over city councils and school boards was hatched by "dominion theologists" with grandiose plans about implementing Biblical law in every sphere of secular society. I first heard about the "county-by-county" stealth takeover plan at the 1986 convention of the Coalition on Revival. COR leaders, among others, were then laying the groundwork for Pat Robertson's 1988 presidential bid. During that effort and the simultaneous TV preacher scandals, the press made laughing stocks of politically active evangelicals. That reinforced the Christian Right's collective martyr complex and the wisdom of stealth strategy.

By 1990, Robertson's Christian Coalition was boasting of its steadily increasing membership rolls while, at the same time, encouraging its local campaign functionaries to keep low profiles lest they be blasted by secular humanists. Through stealth campaigns, the Christian Right won countless elected offices, but the cloak-and-dagger routine also became a public relations liability. Christian Coalition director Ralph Reed made his way-out threats about "flying below radar" and operating like a guerrilla warrior. At best, stealth campaigns can work only for first-time challengers. Increasingly, non-Christian Right voters have become wary of candidates with little-known public policy positions and affiliations.

In 1992, sneaky and undemocratic stealth tactics became the dominant theme in press coverage of the Christian Right. After Clinton's election, the Christian Coalition hired a public relations firm to help the movement project a more "mainstream" image. Recently, Ralph Reed told *Charisma* magazine that he regrets having fostered the stealth model. More significantly, Reed published, in the Heritage Foundation's *Policy Review*, a widely discussed article, "Casting a Wider Net," calling for the Christian Right to broaden its base by granting bottom-line economic concerns as much priority as the "moral" issues. To attract more diverse constituents, the Christian Coalition has also announced its intentions—thus far unrealized—to recruit heavily from minority churches.

Critics of the Christian Right might dismiss Reed's new mainstream soft-sell as the public relations device it most certainly is. But the mainstream gambit has helped the Christian Right solidify alliances with the most dominant faction of the Republican party. After Clinton's election, pundits predicted that moderate Republicans would ditch "extremists" like Pat Robertson. A handful of pro-choice moderates joined forces under former Congress member Tom Campbell's Republican Majority Coalition. Thus far, though, this faction has been unable to wield much influence.

Instead, the most successful new Republican party faction has made clear its intentions to court right-wing evangelicals. In early 1993, Jack Kemp, William J. Bennett, Jeane Kirkpatrick and former Minnesota Congress member Vin Weber launched Empower America. One of their goals has been to dampen Patrick Buchanan's popularity. In the 1992 Republican primaries Buchanan won 25 to 30 percent in most states, largely because of Christian Right backing. Empower America and Buchanan's own American Cause Foundation are diametrically opposed on issues of "free trade" and U.S. military intervention abroad. Both factions seek to represent the Christian Right on the "family values" front but Empower America has a far richer corporate donor base than Buchanan's group. Last fall, Empower America joined forces with the Christian Coalition in the failed effort to pass a "school choice" initiative in California.

Over this and other questions involving the proper role of the state, the Christian Right is divided between those who want to broaden the movement's agenda and those concerned about the pitfalls of collaboration with "mainstream" Republicans. Following Ralph Reed's *Policy Review* article calling for "mainstreaming," the debate went public. In a September *Washington Post* column, Christian Action Network (CAN) president Martin Mawyer chastised Reed for casting too wide a net and, essentially, selling out "pro-family" concerns (abortion, school prayer, opposition to gay rights) to what he called "unrelated" issues like NAFTA and health care reform. In sync with his allies over at Empower America, Reed had endorsed NAFTA though, as Mawyer reports, the audience applauded when Patrick Buchanan denounced NAFTA at a Christian Coalition conference. Mawyer concluded that broadening the Coalition's legislative agenda will not translate into victories on salient "moral" issues.

For its part, CAN has focused on single-issue campaigns. CAN was front-and-center in last year's lobbying to maintain the bans on gay military personnel and on federal funding for poor women's abortions. CAN also took credit for persuading Congress to cut the budget of the National Endowment for the Arts by $8.6 million.

Though CAN opposes subordinating Christian Right activism to the interests of the Republican Party, per se, there is nothing particularly "extreme" about its tactics. CAN uses direct mailing lists to mobilize phone calls and letters to Congress members. That CAN pursues a narrow issue focus and the Christian Coalition hopes to make itself indispensable to the Republican Party is, if anything, a sign of the Christian Right's maturity. Social movements are successful to the extent that activists and leaders with divergent strategies can each find a niche. The public debate between Ralph Reed and Martin Mawyer was inconsequential for a movement that now effectively accommodates both single issue and party-oriented organizations. Both types of groups are successful because they exploit elements of routine electoral politics: Congress members' response to constituent lobbying and persistent low voter turnout, both of which are advantageous to the highly mobilized evangelical minority.

It does no good, then, to see the Christian Right through the blinders of a "radical-extremist" paradigm. It is outrageous that the Right wants to lock gays in closets, deprive women of reproductive freedom, enforce antiquated and monolithic school curricula—the litany is well known. But in the coming season of local and statewide elections, the Christian Right will hold the high ground as well-organized, well-heeled and genuinely discontented opponents of the Clinton era status quo. To crudely blast politically active evangelicals as "extremists" will only increase their claimed underdog status. The only way for opponents to beat back otherwise inevitable Christian Right gains will be to disavow name calling and instead—with cool heads—to conduct grassroots voter education on the true policy aims of the Republican-Christian Right alliance.

Change in Strategy

The Humanist, January/February 1994

The Christian Right's recent overtures to African-American church leaders were punctuated last summer when the San Francisco board of supervisors voted to remove from the city's Human Rights Commission one Rev. Eugene Lumpkin. The prominent black Baptist minister had inflamed public sentiment with his repeated descriptions of homosexuality as "an abomination against God." In the heat of the controversy, Lumpkin told a TV talk show host that he concurred with the Old Testament's prescription of stoning "sodomites" to death. White preachers from the Traditional Values Coalition rallied behind Rev. Lumpkin at a press conference. Charges of homophobia and racism flew fast and furious as the whole incident threatened to rupture alliances between the city's black and gay civil rights advocates. In the end, cooler heads prevailed, but not without raising the specter of the Christian Right's designs on new recruits outside its previous all white base of support. On Lumpkin's behalf, the Rutherford Institute, a Christian Right legal firm, filed a lawsuit against the San Francisco mayor for supposed religious discrimination.

In part the Christian Right's appeal to some black evangelicals is made possible by shared denominational traditions that cross racial lines: Baptists and Pentecostals have more in common with each other than they do with main-line churchgoers irrespective of race. But if shared worship styles were the sole basis for bonds between conservative black clergy and the Christian Right, why, then is an alliance between the two camps emerging only now?

Central to the Christian Right's new quest for racial diversity in its ranks is the drive to split gay rights advocates from their natural allies in communities of color. Black churches have been a mainstay of the African-American civil rights movement. They are now a target of Christian Right propaganda aimed at instilling fear of homosexuals, the latest group to assert its demands for legal equality.

Among the Christian Right's new genre of anti-gay home video cassettes is "Gay Rights, Special Rights: Inside the Homosexual Agenda," produced for the Traditional Values Coalition by Jeremiah Films and designed for an audience concerned about civil rights. The 40-minute scare flick relies heavily on footage from the April 1993 gay-lesbian-bisexual march for equality in Washington, D.C. Featured are the obligatory transvestite strip-tease scenes and countless clips of lip-locked gay and lesbian marchers intercut with shots of young children's angelic faces. This film's variation on a crude theme is the message that gay "special rights" elevate chosen "lifestyles" to the level of immutable racial categories and, thereby, effectively undermine the legitimate minority status of people of color. Mixed with footage from Martin Luther King, Jr.'s famous "I Have a Dream" speech, we hear arguments against gay rights from, among others, two great civil libertarians: former Drug Czar William Bennett and former Attorney General Edwin Meese.

Undoubtedly, the African-American community as a whole is no more homophobic than the white population. Few will be fooled by specious claims that gay rights initiatives will reduce the weight of laws outlawing racial discrimination. In the public relations realm, though, the Traditional Values Coalition and its ilk are counting on support from that small but vocal number of preachers who may use racially charged arguments to disrupt civil rights coalitions in cities where gay rights are controversial.

Beyond this type of opportunism, the Christian Right's new found racial inclusiveness is taking other forms, both cultural and decidedly political. Within the evangelical subculture, black and white church leaders are beginning to communicate openly about racism among Christians. A recent *Christianity Today* cover story, "The Myth of Racial Progress," featured complaints about racism in the church from prominent African-American ministers plus a special message from the magazine's co-founder, Billy Graham. "Racism—in the world and in the church—is one of the greatest barriers to world evangelization," Graham wrote.

Evangelicals' efforts at what they call "racial reconciliation" have been increasingly evident on the pages of *Charisma*, a popular magazine geared less toward clergy and more toward everyday admirers of the leading religious broadcasters. *Charisma*'s own recent cover story, "Healing the Rift Between the Races," profiled some of the largest of the new racially mixed charismatic churches: John Meares' Evangel Temple in Washington, D.C.; Rod Parsley's World Harvest Church in Columbus, Ohio; Benny Hinn's Orlando (Florida) Christian Center; Dick Bernal's Jubilee Christian Center in San Jose, California; Joseph Garlington's Covenant Church of Pittsburgh.

Every month, *Charisma* is loaded with ads for "camp meetings." At these two or three day mini-vacations for born-again Christians, the entertainment is gospel music and high energy preaching by charismatic celebrities. Recently, *Charisma* has advertised a slew of such camp meetings headed by black preachers. More impressively, the events are increasingly inter-racial gatherings. In Tulsa every June, Oral Roberts and the 70-odd "trustees" of his "International Charismatic Bible Ministries" put on one of the biggest of the tent revivals. At that camp meeting, well-known white TV preachers (Oral's son Richard Roberts, Paul Crouch, Kenneth Copeland, Marilyn Hickey, to name a few) share the pulpit with their black counterparts.

The most prominent of these is Carleton Pearson, a graduate and regent of Oral Roberts University. Pearson's racially integrated church is one part of his fast-growing Higher Dimensions Evangelistic Center, based in Tulsa. Pearson's ministry is explicitly aimed at inter-racial recruitment. He calls his travelling revival shows "Azusa Street" crusades, by way of invoking the early history of American pentecostalism. From 1906 to 1913, the "Azusa Street mission" in Los Angeles was led by a black Holiness preacher who drew an inter-racial following.

Among the promotional materials I received from Pearson's headquarters was a brochure listing his counselling center's support groups—including a special one for inter-racial couples and families. The premier edition of Pearson's "Azusa Fire" magazine tells the story of Johnny Lee Clary, a former Ku Klux Klansman and body guard for David Duke, who has now repented for his gruesome past and joined Pearson's integrated church.

Frank discussion of racial bigotry is now a frequent topic on evangelical TV talk shows. Night after night on the two Christian networks my cable service offers (Trinity Broadcasting Network and United Christian Broadcasting), the guest lists are increasingly diverse. Where else but through the multi-billion dollar religious broadcasting industry can up-and-coming black preachers make themselves known to the multitudes? These new faces represent that minority of the African-American church community which is middle class, upwardly mobile and eager to collaborate with conservative politicians.

Carleton Pearson boasts of his past attendance at White House briefings with President George Bush, "in an effort to achieve unity among blacks and conservatives." Southern California's Rev. E.V. Hill, a regular guest on Trinity Broadcasting Network, took to the airwaves to announce his appointment as aide to Los Angeles' new conservative mayor Richard Riordan. Hill's Mt. Zion Missionary Baptist Church lies in riot-damaged south central L.A., and Hill—along with local chapters of the Christian Coalition—backed Riordan's campaign. In return, Riordan authorized Hill to convene a town meeting at which residents were invited to register their suggestions for how the city might solve neighborhood problems. To the extent that Christian Right-linked black preachers make names for themselves on Christian TV, they become—in the eyes of politicians—recognized spokespersons for "their people."

The whole question of who speaks for African Americans was pivotal during Judge Clarence Thomas' Supreme Court nomination in 1991. As part of the Christian Right's efforts to see Thomas confirmed, the Traditional Values Coalition in Washington, D.C., organized pro-Thomas rallies by black clergy. That same summer, in California, TVC's Steve Sheldon told me of his work mobilizing black churches to lobby against a state assembly bill for gay rights.

In these cases, white Christian Right activists allied with black conservatives to make their causes appear more mainstream across racial and class lines. In this vein, the Family Research Council (the lobbying affiliate of Focus on the Family) recently named as vice-president Kay Cole James, a black anti-abortion activist. Like many of the professionals leading Christian Right organizations, James has a track record in government service. In the Bush administration, she served as Assistant Secretary for Public Affairs at the Department of Health and Human Services. Prior to that she was appointed by Reagan to the National Commission on Children and to the 'White House Task Force on the Black Family.

James was one of several African-American speakers at last September's Christian Coalition "Road to Victory" conference. The Christian Coalition makes no secret of its intention to cultivate a mainstream public image. Last summer Christian Coalition executive director Ralph Reed, in a *New York Times* commentary excerpted from a longer article in the Heritage Foundation's *Policy Review*, urged the "pro-family" movement to pay more attention to bottom-line economic concerns affecting middle America: tax cuts, wage increases, and college scholarships. In a recent interview on National Public Radio, Reed elaborated on his goal of broadening the Christian Coalition's base across racial and ethnic lines. In October, the Christian Coalition's publication *Christian American* featured a front-page photo of a young black family next to a report of a poll the Coalition commissioned to show that black and Latino respondents hold conservative views on social issues like abortion, homosexuality, crime, welfare and affirmative action. Reed was quoted to the effect that the Christian Right will no longer "concede the minority community to the political left," and he announced that the Coalition will soon begin advertising on minority-owned radio stations and sending its literature to black and Latino churches.

All of this activity dispels the old stereotype of white fundamentalists as unrepentant racists. It has been easy for critics of the Christian right to point to the movement's lily white membership and say that these people do not come close to representing a diverse and legitimate part of U.S. society. It would be easy now to say that the Christian Right's new found racial inclusiveness is just another public relations ploy, and there is evidence to support such a case. The same October issue of *Christian American* recaps the Christian Coalition's September "Road to Victory" conference. Included among the participant photos is one of Rev. Billy McCormack, a Robertson associate and Coalition board member. Just two years ago, McCormack was an ardent supporter of "former" Klansman David Duke's gubernatorial campaign, as were many Christian Coalition activists. Also on hand, of course, was Senator Jesse Helms who began his activist career years ago as a broadcast journalist and occasional contributor to the monthly magazine of the segregationist white Citizens' Councils.

The old sin of bigotry dies hard, and the Christian Right's new recruitment of black faces says nothing about whether the movement will act in the interests of any but that small number of middle class black church leaders ready to follow their white brethren's lead.

No Place to Hide

The Humanist, September/October 1993

There was one element of surprise in the March 10 murder of Dr. David Gunn by a "pro-life" activist—and that was that it didn't happen sooner.

For more than 20 years, the anti-abortion movement has waged a relentless rhetorical campaign to depict abortion as a Holocaust in progress. Several months after Dr. Gunn's death, it has been sobering—though not surprising—to witness Christian Right leaders' unwillingness to assume any responsibility for the inevitable consequences of their escalated "No Place to Hide" tactics. Since Clinton's election, incidents of clinic vandalism have increased. More ominously, individual local doctors and clinic operators increasingly find themselves and their families threatened with late night phone calls, defamed on posters carrying their photos and home addresses, stalked as they travel from one part of town to another.

Days after the fatal shooting of Dr. Gunn, Christian Coalition executive director Ralph Reed tried his hand at damage control in a guest editorial for the *Wall Street Journal*. Reed called confessed killer Michael Griffin a "ticking time bomb waiting to explode," but then shifted blame for Griffin's deed onto mainstream culture's purported failure to show respect for church-going Americans.

As I write, Operation Rescue has pledged a siege of disruptions at clinics and doctors' homes in half a dozen cities this summer. If future Michael Griffins outside the gates explode like "ticking time bombs," then the Ralph Reeds, Pat Robertsons and Randall Terrys will bear part of the responsibility. The anti-abortionists have lost the initiative at the federal level, yet the movement's leaders continue to court violence by inciting their most militant foot soldiers.

This year cities and counties around the country have passed ordinances to restrict aggressive picketing outside clinics and doctors' homes. Attorney General Janet Reno backs a proposed

Freedom of Access to Clinic Entrances Act that would make it a federal crime to block access to abortion clinics. Such a law would complement the Freedom of Choice Act, currently making its way through Congress, which would effectively codify *Roe v. Wade* by precluding states from passing excessive legal restrictions. Together the two pieces of federal legislation would go a long way toward protecting abortion rights, in theory and in practice.

Before concluding that legal measures will stop anti-abortion harassment, however, we might consider the Christian Right's strengths and weaknesses on this front. How has the anti-abortion movement arrived at its current emphasis on targeting doctors? Through what avenues, legal and otherwise, does the movement plan to continue its "No Place to Hide" strategy?

For two decades, the general public has remained predominantly pro-choice while the anti-abortionists have steadily upped the ante. Ronald Reagan campaigned on the idea that he would promote anti-abortion legislation in Congress and stack the Supreme Court for the eventual overturn of *Roe v. Wade*. In Congress, the "Human Life Amendment" went nowhere, and the judicial appointment process proved too slow for Christian Right zealots. As early as 1982, a rash of clinic bombings began. Then Reagan was reelected with large backing from the Christian Right while, according to statistics compiled by the National Abortion Federation, the number of bombings, arsons, death threats and incidents of vandalism rose sharply between 1984 and 1986. Still, the Reagan administration remained less than 100 percent willing and able to outlaw abortion. But neither was the government committed to any serious effort to stop clinic violence. In one well-publicized case, two young couples from Pensacola, Florida, were prosecuted for three 1984 Christmas eve clinic bombings. Their story is told in a highly recommended new book, *Religious Violence and Abortion: The Gideon Project*, by Dallas A. Blanchard and Terry J. Prewitt, (University Press of Florida). But their case was exceptional. Countless clinic bombers got away, and the obvious message was that women's clinics were fair game for terrorists.

By contrast, during the mid-1980s, the FBI devoted sizeable

resources to busting up an Aryan Nations subgroup known as "the Order." Granted, this small band of violent neo-Nazis assassinated a radio talk show host and killed several federal marshals in the line of duty. Aggressive anti-abortionists were potentially no less of a terrorist threat, yet the Reagan-Bush administrations turned a blind eye to the movement's escalation.

In 1988 Crossway Books, a major evangelical publisher, released *A Pro-Life Manifesto*. The book expounded on the possibilities of waging "armed aggression" against abortion. Here's a sample of the book's tenor:

> If armed aggression were the answer, it would have to be aggression that did not hesitate. It would have to be done on a large scale, and more than a few abortion clinics would have to be destroyed. To succeed, it would require the destruction of all hospitals or clinics that performed abortions. Heroes who would lay down their life for the cause would have to come forth. Armies would need to be organized. Companies producing abortifacients would have to be bombed and their employees terrorized. In short, we would have to be willing to plunge ourselves into civil war.

> While at times it seems that we are headed for just such a scenario, the conditions are not right for that to happen. The pro-life forces don't have the aggressive, radical leadership necessary to accomplish that goal. There is not enough cohesion in the pro-life camp. We don't have the masses of people who are so enraged that they would sacrifice all to further this cause. No, the pro-life leadership is bound to work within the system. It will not take up this cause, even though it is much more urgent than the cause that started the Civil War, because the zeal is not there that was present then.

Short of outright civil war, however, aggressive anti-abortionists were prepared to escalate their tactics in other ways. Their handbook was Joseph Scheidler's *Closed: 99 Ways to Stop Abortion*, (also published by Crossway Books) which instructed activists in the means to harass clinic providers, pro-choice groups and women seeking abortions.

Scheidler was an inspiration to Randall Terry, who launched

Operation Rescue in May 1988 with a week of clinic blockades in New York City. Operation Rescue won the endorsement of respected Christian Right figures, including Pat Robertson, Jerry Falwell, James Dobson, Beverly LaHaye and Cardinal John J. O'Connor. In turn, Operation Rescue leaders were careful not to claim tactical supremacy over fellow anti-abortionists using more moderate, legal tactics. Operation Rescue stayed both militant and well-integrated into the multi-faceted Christian Right, and that helped OR grow as a grassroots phenomenon. In 1990, when a U.S. attorney's office seized OR's financial assets and Randall Terry was forced to close his Binghamton, New York office rather than pay a $50,000 settlement in a suit brought by the National Organization for Women, the "rescue movement" decentralized and went on its merry way. OR headquarters relocated to South Carolina and stopped soliciting funds that could wind up in the hands of suing plaintiffs. Instead, about 100 small, autonomous "rescue" organizations remained loosely connected. Terry and others formed the Christian Defense Coalition to recruit "pro-life" attorneys to defend clinic blockaders in the courts.

Meanwhile, pro-choice people also got smarter. After anti-abortion demonstrators shut down clinics in Witchita in the summer of 1991, Operation Rescue met its match in the streets of Buffalo, New York. There a valiant pro-choice coalition defeated OR's "Spring of Life" campaign and kept the clinics open. Here in northern California since 1988, the Bay Area Coalition for Our Reproductive Rights (BACORR) has sent teams of clinic defenders to meet Operation Rescue blockaders every step of the way. No laws, no public opinion polls stop Operation Rescue. Only through collective determination—and careful analysis of the anti-abortionists' latest plans—does BACORR get its activists out of bed hours before sunrise and in front of targeted clinics before OR arrives.

Only after BACORR and its counterparts elsewhere have demonstrated their resolve to keep clinics open have various city councils enacted so-called "bubble laws" to restrict residential picketing and to keep anti-abortion protesters at least eight feet away from clinic entrances. Civil libertarians worry about the bubble laws' First Amendment implications. Like it or not, anti-abortionists have free speech rights, too.

Yet with each new phase of the abortion struggle, the anti-choicers have accommodated. It's not hard to imagine how OR's far-flung affiliates—stuck for long hours outside clinics and in jails—came up with the idea of attacking doctors in the latest "No Place to Hide" campaign. Repeatedly, Randall Terry has proclaimed that "the doctor is the weak link" in abortion accessibility. Large clinic blockades carry obvious disadvantages, namely successful counter-protests, jail time and fines. Direct attacks on clinics and doctors are legally more risky for perpetrators but likewise more threatening to pro-choicers.

Though anti-abortionists might not like to admit it, their evident shift away from massive blockades and toward pointed attacks on doctors reflects a recognition that the battle for public opinion is at a stalemate. Polls show majority public sentiment to be generally pro-choice. But on either side of the issue, only tiny minorities feel strong enough to take to the streets. From a pro-choice perspective, then, there's a down side to the anti-choicers' likely retreat from the large demonstration tactic: Should Operation Rescue's "Cities of Refuge" siege fizzle this summer, the mainstream media will pronounce the anti-abortion movement dead in the water—and plenty of pro-choicers will agree.

That kind of dangerous illusion will do nothing to stop the anti-abortionists' sub rosa escalation. They are honing their skills as spies and saboteurs for guerrilla warfare against doctors and pro-choice advocates. The most militant "rescuers" may actually prefer not to demonstrate in front of clinics and TV news cameras. From the theory of "armed aggression" and Joseph Scheidler's handy harassment tips, the "pro-lifers" are now circulating covert operations manuals such as the California branch of Operation Rescue's *Abortion Buster's Manual*. First self-published by a Kevin Sherlock of southern California in 1985, the manual now has a readership ready to apply its lessons.

The booklet teaches anti-abortion investigators the basics of private sleuthing.

> Why should pro-lifers get involved in this kind of work? Because it will damage the abortionists! For the last dozen years since Roe vs. Wade, pro-lifers have been able to

show without question that abortion on demand kills innocent unborn human beings. However, this has not restored the protection of the law to the unborn. Instead, most people could care less, and the people in the pro-abortion camp have proven their minds and hearts are resistant to logic and fairness. So we have to add new tactics to our fight. We can use the huge amount of negative info that exists on abortionists as a weapon to run a few of them, then some more of them, then a whole lot of them out of the abortion business. If it becomes too much of a hassle to run an abortion mill, then fewer people will do it, and the number of abortions will drop. We might not be able to cut off the enemy's head yet, but we can certainly start making him bleed from a number of wounds.

From there, the *Abortion Buster's Manual* instructs readers to pose as neutral or pro-choice while gathering documentary evidence about abortion providers from clinics and public records offices. The techniques described are exhaustive: Call a clinic to get the name of its private insurance company. Then call the insurer and tell them you're a policy holder looking for the name of a local abortion doctor. Check the OB/GYN offices of private and county hospitals to find out where else a given doctor may work during the week. Pretend to be a salesperson peddling magazines or medical supplies and ask the clinic receptionist for each doctor's name so you can send "sample products." Use friends in local police departments or vehicle registration agencies to run license plate checks for home addresses.

Most of the techniques described in the *Abortion Buster's Manual* are technically legal, though obviously of questionable "morality." Nor is Operation Rescue alone in its current emphasis on investigating doctors. Focus on the Family projects itself as the most moderate and reasonable part of the Christian Right apparatus. The June issue of Focus on the Family's monthly *Citizen* magazine includes "Pro-life Strategies in Hard Times," on tactics for scaring doctors away from performing abortions. The article urges pro-life advocates to "turn up the heat" by proposing state regulatory legislation that, for starters, would require abortion doctors to carry expensive malpractice and liability insurance policies and that would require clinics to maintain on-site emergency medical equipment with staff certified to use it. On the lawsuit front, Focus recommends that anti-abortionists hook up with a Pensacola-based outfit, Legal Action for Women. This network of "pro-life" lawyers recruits women who regret their abortions and want to sue doctors for big bucks. Along the same lines, Focus recommends the American Rights Coalition, a clearinghouse for "pro-lifers" working to get local abortion doctors' licenses revoked. Finally, Focus on the Family suggests that pro-lifers pool their money to buy up the buildings where abortion doctors practice and then, of course, evict them.

These and other nasty tricks can be used against anyone who speaks out on behalf of women's rights. In anticipation of Operation Rescue's summer "Cities of Refuge" blitzkrieg, a friend of mine who hosts a radio talk show invited a couple of pro-choice activists onto the airwaves. For her trouble, she found herself stalked by a thug from Operation Rescue. He trailed her into a public building and held her against her will while he babbled Bible verses and demanded to know if she's a lesbian.

What ought to concern pro-choicers is the anti-abortion movement's transformation into an extra-legal intelligence gathering unit with the propensity to act on the information it compiles. What are the limits if anti-abortionists make their crusade increasingly personal and vindictive?

Televangelists
Singin' the Blues

Z Magazine, April 1993

The fiftieth anniversary convention of the National Religious Broadcasters association should have been a time for its 5,000 participants to celebrate. The multi-billion dollar a year Christian broadcast industry survived the debilitating TV preacher scandals of 1987 and 1988. The number of Christian TV and radio stations has remained stable, while the expansion of cable TV has fostered the growth of two thriving networks: the New Inspirational Network, with 550 affiliate cable systems syndicating 18 of the most popular TV preachers; and Pat Robertson's Family Channel, featuring his own "700 Club" talk show plus round-the-clock "family" oriented entertainment.

But the mood of this year's convention, held for the first time in Los Angeles, rather than in Washington, D.C., was somber and fearful. Leaders of the Christian Right conveyed serious trepidation about an administration they consider demonically inspired. Diminished in political power at the national level, they vowed to wage a "cultural war," not only by continuing to elect candidates to local government offices, but also through a subtle redeployment of their propaganda skills and assets. If nothing else, the Christian Right's flexible strategy is a sign of the movement's sophistication and endurance.

Dialing for Jesus

Minus a presidential campaign or a juicy "fundamentalist" scandal-in-progress, this year, the secular press—with the exception of *Z Magazine*—was conspicuously absent from NRB's convention. No longer do flamboyant personalities like Jimmy Swaggart and Jerry Falwell dominate the religious broadcasting scene and attract a press room full of reporters eager for a quick, fun story on those crazy TV preachers. Instead, less than a year after the hot days of rebellion in the nation's entertainment industry capitol, local broadcast news was fixated on the mid-February Academy Award nominations.

At the L.A. Convention Center and its nearby plush hotels, the religious broadcasters held their own awards ceremonies. At the opening session, "Beverly La Haye Live," started in 1990 and now airing on 60 radio stations, won the 1993 "Talk Show of the Year" award for its "outstanding achievement" on political issues. Mrs. La Haye's Concerned Women for America claims credit for stalling passage of the Freedom of Choice Act last year by "bombarding" Congress with 30,000 telegrams from radio listeners.

The second evening's session, "Hollywood Night," was a tribute to evangelicals employed in the entertainment industry. Dr. Lloyd Ogilvie told how his Hollywood Presbyterian Church evangelizes local movie actors, writers and producers. Pat Boone, tanned and youthful as ever, treated the crowd of 1,000 to his new song "Can't We Get Along?" a sappy paraphrase of Rodney King's televised press conference last year. Daughter Debbie Boone accepted kudos for her work as mother of four and belted out the theme song from the "Sound of Music."

Small daytime convention workshops were devoted to the nitty gritty of hustling "the gospel." At a session on "TV Fundraising for the '90s," "700 Club" executive producer Norm Mintle shared the Christian Broadcasting Network's goal of relying less on semi-annual telethons. Gary Evans, of the Russ Reid "direct response marketing" agency in Pasadena, explained how World Vision and some of his other clients raise hundreds of millions of dollars annually. The first step is to get a TV host who can speak smoothly without looking like he's reading from a teleprompter. "We don't believe in ad libbing. Every word is scripted." But the trick, Evans said, is not to expect large sums from one-time viewers who are moved to get off the couch and dial a toll-free number. Successful program content is nothing but a "donor acquisition tool." "You're acquiring names and that's all," said Evans. "Your real fundraising is done by direct mail— later." The direct mail campaigns are built around an "exchange" or an "offer," either "tangible things or felt benefits" that the viewer will feel the need to buy. Evans stressed the need to "package" the "exchange" in precise terms: 50 dollars will go to purchase X pounds of rice. The secret, Evans said, is to keep the "package" simple and as non-controversial as possible.

Storming the Gates

Likewise, simplicity is the name of the game for Pat Robertson's latest media venture. Last spring Robertson made a bid to purchase the ailing United Press International but then decided that the costs needed to refurbish the wire service were too high. Instead, Robertson has recently launched *Standard News*, a Washington, D.C.-based satellite service accessible to 1,200 Christian radio stations. *Standard News* offers subscribers two daily "feeds" featuring a two-minute Christian-oriented newscast, "The Rest of the News" and a package of pre-recorded commentaries, feature stories and interviews for station managers to mix and match as they like.

Internationally, Robertson's Christian Broadcasting Network continues to broadcast in 35 countries. The affiliated Middle East Television, headquartered on the Israel-Lebanon border, is in its eleventh year of broadcasting and is in the vanguard of the Christian Right's new preoccupation with the growth of Islamic fundamentalism.

This year's NRB convention workshop on "the Islamic threat" stressed the post-Gulf War concern with the problem among U.S. foreign policymakers and the mainstream media. The evangelicals link the religious fervor of countries like Saudi Arabia and Iran to potentially increasing hostility toward U.S. oil interests. Annis Shorrosh, a Palestinian Christian from Nazareth, directed all the workshop participants to kneel Muslim-style and pray for the salvation of the Arab world. Among the speakers urging born-agains to take their crusade to the Muslim countries, Gerald Derstine of Bradenton, Florida, had the most curious stories to tell. During the 1980s, Derstine's son Phil was a collaborator in Oliver North's network of born-again fundraisers for the Nicaraguan contras. Derstine Senior makes frequent trips to visit with Israeli government officials, and he's an avid recruiter of pro-Israeli Palestinians living on the West Bank and Gaza strip. Derstine claims to have been the target of countless assassination attempts by Muslim "terrorists," all of whom have miraculously repented and surrendered to Jesus Christ.

The Horns of the Anti-Christ

Among all the "pro-lifers," only about 30 of the 5,000 NRB conventioneers bothered to attend a Monday evening workshop on "The Pro-Life Movement Under President Clinton." The event featured Dr. John Willke, the Ohio pediatrician who founded the National Right to Life Committee in 1973. Willke recently left his legislative lobbying in Washington, D.C., and returned to Cincinnati to launch the Life Issues Institute, a think tank devoted to producing "educational" themes and materials for the anti-abortion movement.

Willke told an apocryphal story bound to become a classic among the Christian Right. It seems that on the morning of Clinton's inauguration, a "pro-life" activist named Lureen managed to get past a White House security guard and seat herself in the third row of a church service behind Bill and Hillary Clinton. As Bill came down the aisle and shook Lureen's hand, she told him: "God doesn't want you to kill unborn babies." He gave her a blank stare and kept moving. Next, Hillary hugged her, and Lureen repeated: "God doesn't want you to kill unborn babies." Hillary stood back and let go of Lureen. Then Hillary's countenance changed to that of a person seemingly possessed, and she responded: "It is God's law to kill babies."

Such was the tone of the rest of Willke's presentation. Beyond Clinton's immediate executive orders lifting the gag order on abortion referrals at federally funded family planning clinics, allowing for the importation of RU-486 and authorizing fetal tissue research, Willke braced "pro-lifers" for further impending atrocities. He predicted that the administration will try to destroy the movement's 3,000 "crisis pregnancy centers" through regulatory requirements that they meet the standards of emergency room facilities. The Democrats, he said, will change the rules on political action committee donations to restrict the flow of money to anti-abortion Congressmembers, and the Federal Election Commission will begin busting tax-exempt churches for partisan electioneering. The biggest fear—and one that prompted a formal resolution by the National Religious Broadcasters—is that the Federal Communications Commission, under Clinton, will reinstate the "fairness doctrine." That might require Christian TV and radio stations to provide an "opposing viewpoint" every time they use the public airwaves to lobby or spread lies about homosexuals, Planned Parenthood, and other arch-nemeses.

Willke likened anti-abortionists' predicament to that of the anti-slavery movement in the years between its initial growth from the 1830s to the 1850s and the "dark years" prior to the 1860 election of Abraham Lincoln. Right now, Willke said, the "pro-aborts" have seized the moral high ground by shifting the terms of debate from "is abortion murder?" to the question of "who decides." Through polling, Willke's Life Issues Institute has concluded that the majority of people uncommitted on legal abortion still think a woman has the ultimate right to decide. The solution, therefore, is for "pro-lifers" to move away from confrontation, to start showing they care and, as Willke put it, to "start oozing compassion for women. Our Christian media has to sound that trumpet almost ad nauseum."

A "Persecuted" Majority

At the same time, the Christian Right has established several law firms to protect the civil rights of "persecuted" Christians. Of the two represented at booths in the convention exhibit hall, the newest and most ambitious is the American Center for Law and Justice (ACLJ), founded by Pat Robertson and housed at his Virginia Beach headquarters. Headed by Jew-for-Jesus attorney Jay Sekulow, the ACLJ won a recent Supreme Court case on behalf of Operation Rescue. The Court rejected arguments by Planned Parenthood, the National Organization for Women, et al., that abortion clinic blockaders target women as a special "class."

Active since 1982, the Rutherford Institute represents a variety of Christian "civil liberties" litigants: anti-abortion demonstrators, students asked not to read Bibles at public schools, parents whose home school facilities fail to meet government regulations. No doubt, Christians deserve as much legal protection as anyone else. But with much of the ACLJ and Rutherford case load, there's a fine line between defending the interests of clients and stepping on the rights of other people. In a recent commentary sent to Christian radio stations, Rutherford Institute president John Whitehead argues that workplace seminars on gay rights are a form of "religious discrimination" against employees who are "told to rid themselves of stereotypes about gays and to accept homosexuality as a valid lifestyle choice." In an odd assertion of victim status, Whitehead claims Christian military personnel may jeopardize their careers if they "speak out against homosexuality....The immediate remedy is for the military to exempt religious people from compelled personal acceptance of homosexuality."

The Rutherford Institute extends the concept of "religious discrimination" to its own movie review of Steve Martin's latest comedy. "Leap of Faith" is a spoof on the classic "Marjoe" and "Elmer Gantry" type characters who use flashy tent revivals to bilk a gullible audience. Unable to crack a smile, Rutherford's magazine reviewer charges the film with "silly humanism" for its presentation of "religion and everything associated with it, good or bad, as stemming from man [sic]."

The movie industry's unflattering portrayal of church-based "money changers" is a major irritant to film critic Michael Medved. His book *Hollywood vs. America* is an elaborate conspiracy theory to the effect that the entertainment industry violates its own profit motive in order to ram sexually threatening imagery down the throats of decent Americans. According to Medved, the public hungers for a steady flow of Disney animation films, but movie producers shun these box office hits because the industry's "cultural elitists" favor an unending barrage of obscenity. Medved's tortured statistics and pseudo-logic have made him the Hollywood darling of the Christian Right.

Medved was a featured speaker at the NRB convention's general session on television. There, in the convention press releases and in the association's own *Religious Broadcasting* magazine, the evangelicals gave special recognition to Medved's Jewishness. (He presides over Venice, California's Pacific Jewish Center, which draws secular Jews back to a religious lifestyle.) Medved basked in the warm glow of the evangelicals' fascination with him, while he lamented Hollywood's purported portrayal of religious people as if "we all have hair on our arms and clothes from K-Mart." Medved urged his Christian counterparts to continue their pressure on the entertainment moguls. He gave particular praise to Ted Baehr of the Christian Film and Television Commission, a coalition of NRB leaders who support the reinstatement of the old "Motion Picture and Television Code" that disallowed obscenity, nudity and sex scenes, detailed portrayal of violence, and derogatory use of religious symbology.

Dinner with Pat

Michael Medved was a special guest at the NRB convention's final evening banquet at the swank Hilton hotel. There I dined and made small talk with two ultra-polite couples who evidenced little interest in my Z Magazine press badge. From Pittsburgh, Chuck manages two Christian radio stations and his chatterbox wife Susan raises their two sons. Paul and Miriam are Brazilian missionaries who pastor a church of 200 mostly Mexican immigrant converts in Orange County. Miriam spoke only under the approving gaze of her zealous husband-preacher, who charmed the rest of us at the table with stories of "the Lord's work" among southern California's Spanish-speaking population.

The highlight of the three-hour musical, oratory—but not culinary—extravaganza was the keynote speech by Pat Robertson. It was vintage hellfire and brimstone. Robertson declined to boast of the phenomenal growth of his Christian Coalition. With 700 chapters throughout all 50 states and "training schools" convened in 70 cities in recent months, this organization represents the Christian Right's most serious effort yet to build an indispensable Republican Party faction. Pat wasted no time congratulating himself. Instead, he cut right to the chase.

"We have entered a time of moral conflict that is hitherto unknown to our nation," Robertson told his brethren, whom he referred to as "a royal priesthood." He cited the latest statistics on crime, incarceration rates, juvenile delinquency, illegitimate births, and AIDS cases." Every indice of our national health is in decline," he said. But "the answer is not more tax and spend liberalism of the welfare state."

Robertson then fixed his attention on the question of gays in the military. "Instead of compelling the armed forces to accept homosexuals, I would call on the president to take a stand against the ungodly lifestyle that destroys all it touches." Robertson recounted how in February he had done his "civic duty" by broadcasting the phone number for the Capitol switchboard, generating tens of thousands of calls from Christians against Clinton's proposed lifting of the ban on gay military personnel. When the *Washington Post* reported—inaccurately—that the evangelical phone callers "are largely poor, uneducated and easy to command," Robertson read the ill-informed article over the air, flashed the *Post*'s address and suggested that viewers list their incomes and university degrees in their protest letters. The *Washington Post* was embarrassed into retracting reporter Michael Weisskopf's idiotic assertions.

Finally, Robertson urged the NRB crowd to continue to "mobilize churches in concert" in order to elect people to offices from the school board to the House of Representatives. "We don't have to be under the rule of people who engage in bizarre activity," Robertson said. "We can cry out to God for a mighty spiritual awakening in this nation." The seven years from now until the end of this millennium are "crucial for the destiny of America." By the year 2000, Robertson prayed, Christians will look back and say: "We didn't fail. God through his grace gave us this land."

Part II
"Ideas Have Consequences"

Readin', Writin' and Repressin'

Z Magazine, February 1991

In the mind-set of right-wing strategists, academia is hotly contested terrain, and the stakes couldn't be higher. Who will decide what versions of reality young people will be exposed to? Who will become the officially recognized "experts" advising policymakers in government and influencing public opinion via the mass media? A large cohort of white men holding sway over academia since the 1950s is now retiring, and many of their seats are being filled by women and people of color. The more diverse the student body and faculty become, the more out-moded curricula inevitably—and justifiably—will be called into question.

It is precisely at this time that the Right has revived its long-standing concern with purported leftist domination of academia. The demise of "international communism" as an adversarial preoccupation leaves right-wing intellectuals with an obvious target of next resort: the liberals and radicals who've managed to hold some ground during the dark ages of the Reagan-Bush administrations' education budget cuts.

Case Study: University of Texas, Austin

The National Association of Scholars (NAS) is leading the drive to preserve academia's preferential option for all that's rich, white, macho and ancient. NAS has been particularly active at the University of Texas at Austin, site of a full-scale right-wing backlash.

Last spring, the Texas chapter of NAS emerged in reaction to proposed changes in a lower division writing course. Amidst a climate of increasing racial and sexual harassment at UT, English professor Linda Brodkey proposed that E306 be revised to include readings about civil rights issues, from a sociology textbook on race and gender. The idea was to give students provocative and socially relevant themes around which they would construct their own written arguments. Among the English department faculty, opinion was divided, but before any compromise could be reached, the campus Right took the proposal and ran with it.

Two Texas NAS members, Professor Alan Gribben from the English Department and Philosophy Professor Daniel Bonevac, made wild allegations about leftist "indoctrination" plots. During a local PBS television debate, Bonevac charged that E306 should really be called "Marxism 306." Heritage Foundation syndicated columnist William Murchison was drafted to write biting columns for the *Dallas Morning News*. By summer's end the course revisions—intended to be in place for the Fall 1990 semester—had been postponed for at least a year. In September the English department faculty voted to accept the revised course, pending approval by the dean of the College of Liberal Arts and the University President. In its Fall 1990 newsletter, NAS claimed victory in "resisting a powerful attempt to distort and politicize the curriculum."

While embroiled in the English department fracas, the Texas Association of Scholars also held its first public event in March 1990, a conference entitled "Ideologically-based Suppression of Research in Social Science." Exhibit A of the "suppressed" scholars was TAS chapter head Joseph Horn, a psychology professor who peddles theories on ethnic group differences in intelligence. Horn was then also an assistant dean in the College of Liberal Arts and the faculty adviser to UT's Young Conservatives. Horn encouraged the student rightists to hold rallies and circulate petitions against a Black Student Association proposal to hire more tenured Black faculty and to require all students to take three hours of African or African-American studies. The Chicano student newspaper *Tejas* published an investigative report on Horn's political and academic career and an editorial calling for his resignation as dean. Horn's student group then launched a campaign to protest university funding of *Tejas*. The administration caved in and decided that state funding may be used to write, edit, and publish 50 copies of the paper—one for each class member and the journalism faculty—but not the total circulation of about 5,000 for the student body. The other three journalism class publications received no such treatment.

The incidents at UT suggest that right-wing strategy for academia has moved from an early phase, in the 1980s, of funding likeminded professors and student projects and harassing progressive faculty to confrontations of a more profound and conceptual nature. Now the target is the very idea of using civil rights literature to teach writing skills; or the very idea of a journalism course offering publishing experience for groups under-represented in corporate media. The Right consistently claims to oppose what it calls "the politicization of the academy." Translated, that means opposition to what the left calls "diversity" and "multiculturalism."

Origin of the Species

The National Association of Scholars is the first concerted effort to organize right-wing faculty. NAS began in 1987, but its genealogy can be traced to the Institute for Educational Affairs, founded in 1978 by neoconservative writer Irving Kristol and former Treasury Secretary William Simon. IEA has since served as a conduit for corporate funding of selected academics. (In September 1990, IEA changed its name to the Madison Center for Educational Affairs.)

IEA-Madison Center is bankrolled by corporate foundations, including Coors, Mobil, Smith-Richardson, Earhart, Scaife and Olin. IEA board members—some of whom are also trustees of the contributing foundations—dole out respectable sums to up-and-coming graduate students and junior faculty, according to the minutes of one IEA meeting, "in order to give their work impact and promote their careers."

From the start, IEA differed from an "Old Right" academic project, the Intercollegiate Studies Institute, started in 1952 by associates of William F. Buckley. ISI continues to hold conferences and publish a slew of journals, but the articles are too philosophical and lackluster to attract much attention.

IEA is the force behind a crop of 60 provocative tabloids published on 57 campuses. The most notorious, the *Dartmouth Review*, has repeatedly drawn fire for its bigoted invectives. In 1986, on Martin Luther King, Jr.'s birthday, *Review* staffers tore down shanties built by the college's anti-apartheid groups. In a stunt timed for the 1990 Jewish Yom Kippur holiday, the *Review* published a quotation from Hitler's *Mein Kampf* on its masthead. Dartmouth president James Freedman responded by denouncing the paper—and its outside agitators William F. Buckley, Pat Buchanan, George Gilder and William Rusher—in a *New York Times* op-ed. But while the spotlight has been fixed on IEA's irritating student press, its intellectual authors have quietly laid the groundwork for more insidious means of putting liberal and progressive academics on the defensive.

Behind the Supply Lines

According to a set of documents I've obtained, the immediate predecessor to the NAS was a group called the Campus Coalition for Democracy, headquartered, like NAS, in Princeton. The Coalition began in 1982 and was headed by Stephen H. Balch, a professor of government at the City University of New York. (Balch later became President of NAS.) In 1983 the Campus Coalition held a conference at Long Island University, attended by about 120 people. The subject was Central America and the list of speakers was impressive. Jeane Kirkpatrick gave the plenary address. Panel speakers included Assistant Secretary of State Elliot Abrams, Penn Kemble of the Institute on Religion and Democracy, Michael Ledeen of the Center for Strategic and International Studies, William Doherty of the American Institute for Free Labor Development (AIFLD), and Contra leader Arturo Cruz. The conference program acknowledged funding from the Long Island University John P. McGrath Fund and from the Committee for the Free World.

The Committee for the Free World, headed by Elliott Abrams' mother-in-law Midge Decter, was at the time one of the most important assets in the Reagan administration's war against Nicaragua. It turns out that CFW was also involved in securing funding for the nascent faculty organizing projects. Campus Coalition president Stephen Balch solicited advice from CFW's Steven Munson on getting money from IEA.

By late 1984, the campus organizing plan was spelled out in a confidential memo, "The Report on the Universities" written by Roderic R. Richardson for the Smith-Richardson Foundation.

(It's worth noting that this foundation has had a history of sponsoring CIA-linked media projects and leadership training programs for CIA and Defense Department personnel.) The document proposed to distinguish between two possible anti-left strategies: "deterrence activism" and "highground articulation," also termed "idea marketing." Deterrence activism, wrote Richardson,

> exists purely in response to the left-wing agenda. It is not very interesting, frankly, boring, and it is the kind of activism sponsored heretofore. At best it is a form of   cheerleading that can focus some attention on stirring media events.

Instead, Richardson advocated "highground activism" or "articulation,"

> the attempt to steal one or another highground away from the left, by both action, and articulation. As noted, it involves doing things like insisting on rigorous discussion and debates, setting up political unions, battling divestiture and other causes, not by calling their goals wrong, necessarily, but by proposing better ways of solving the problem. Student journalism is a highground approach....

Richardson recommended that the Right "mimic left-wing organization" by forming what he called Regional Resource Centers, starting with a faculty network

> in one area of the country, say, New England or around New York. The aim of such a group is to set up a permanent network, to defuse the left, to grab the highground, to change the atmosphere on campuses, and perhaps, to help command a corner of the national agenda.

Richardson wrote that he already had support for his plan, but he warned that "the New Right, perceiving a vacuum, might well try to take over the student activist and journalism movements."

The Usual Suspects

Before the Regional Resource Center plan could get off the ground, a faction further to the Right than Richardson and IEA launched Accuracy in Academia. A spin-off of Reed Irvine's Accuracy in Media, AIA recruited classroom spies and began compiling a data base on professors AIA labeled "left-wing propagandists." AIA's first executive director, Les Csorba, was a 22-year-old activist fresh from the University of California at Davis, where he had organized a harassment campaign against visiting lecturer Saul Landau in 1985. AIA President John LeBoutillier, a former member of Congress, was then a leader within the World Anti-Communist League (WACL), as were three other members of AIA's initial advisory board. Irvine himself had at one time been prominent within WACL. At the time of AIA's founding in 1985, WACL was one of the most important coordinating bodies for death squad activities in Central America and elsewhere.

Not because of these connections, but because of its pit bull tactics, AIA attracted plenty of media attention and earned itself a reputation as campus "thought police."

Among AIA's strongest detractors were fellow rightists, including Midge Decter of the Committee for the Free World. In a December 1985 *New York Times* op-ed, Decter expressed agreement with Irvine's view of the professoriate, but charged AIA with mimicking 1960s radicals who had turned the universities into "a veritable hotbed of reckless, mindless anti-Americanism." Advocating the "highground" strategy of her colleagues at the Smith-Richardson Foundation, Decter wrote, "The only way to deal with words and ideas and teachings one deplores is to offer better words and ideas and teachings."

Decter projected herself as a true believer in "academic freedom" when, in fact, she and her ilk were motivated less by civil libertarianism than by the shrewd understanding that the most effective ideological warfare strategy is that which sneaks up on its enemy slowly. AIA was such a crude and noisy operation that it might have discredited—and thereby slowed—other right-wing strategies.

But not for long. In 1986, Decter's *Commentary* magazine published an important article "The Tenured Left" by Stephen H.

Balch and Herbert I. London (who in 1987 would become the founders of the National Association of Scholars). Balch was then associate professor of government at the John Jay College of Criminal Justice in New York. Herbert London was, and is, dean of the Gallatin Division of New York University, as well as a fellow of the Pentagon-funded Hudson Institute in Indiana. Balch and London expressed their distaste for Accuracy in Academia by making a phony analogy between it and the campus anti-apartheid movement. The only difference, as far as Balch and London could see, was that AIA's efforts, "unlike those of the divestiture campaign, have been wholly confined to the realm of public criticism, neither fomenting disruption, nor toying with the possibilities of violent confrontation, nor obliging university administrators or faculty members to adopt an institutional stand."

Their argument continued: anti-apartheid protesters were getting slaps on the wrists, while AIA activists were labeled troublemakers. And all because the academy is dominated by leftists. Among the "evidence" presented, Balch and London reported an incident in 1985 when the *American Sociological Review* had given its lead article space to a real live Marxist—who also happened to be an associate editor of the journal. The Marxist in question was U.C. Berkeley sociologist Michael Burawoy. Balch and London trashed Burawoy's field study of a Hungarian manufacturing plant, because the work was done in collaboration with Janos Lukacs, of the Hungarian Academy of Sciences. The logic was that Burawoy's work could not be scientifically valid so long as his fellow sociologist was a citizen in a communist regime. (Presumably, Balch and London would now approve work by Burawoy and Lukacs, since Hungary's turn toward capitalism.)

Still, the tactic was to red-bait particular scholars. By 1987, the Right's anti-progressive argument was broadened with the publication of Allan Bloom's bestseller, *The Closing of the American Mind*. With generous funding from the Earhart and Olin foundations, Bloom's book constructed a case against the concept of "cultural relativism," propagated by leftist intellectuals, but manifested throughout society in everything from too little Bible reading to too much rock-n-roll. Bloom attributed the dumbing-down of the U.S. citizenry to a gradual erosion of ethnocentric prejudices. "Cultural relativism," he wrote, "succeeds in destroying the West's universal or intellectually imperialistic claims, leaving it to be just another culture."

Enter NAS

In late 1987 the National Association of Scholars (NAS) was formally inaugurated, with Herbert London named Chair of the Board and Stephen Balch, President. Among the prominent board members are Leslie Lenkowsky, formerly research director of the Smith-Richardson Foundation, who was at one time Acting Director of the U.S. Information Agency. Lenkowsky directed IEA until 1990, when he left to become president of the Hudson Institute, the current hang-out for former Drug Czar William Bennett.

A preliminary survey of tax returns from some of the same right-wing foundations bankrolling IEA shows NAS with an annual budget well in excess of a quarter of a million dollars.

The first few issues of NAS' quarterly journal *Academic Questions* took aim at feminist scholarship, affirmative action, supposed leftist control of Latin American, African and Asian studies programs, and even student evaluations of professors. Recent articles are more broad-brushed in approach. One six-page article lamented college students' use of highlighter pens. Beyond its surface absurdity, the real point of the article was that students should not be so free to pick and choose what *they think* they need to remember from any assigned reading. The argument underlying a Fall 1990 article on "the radical politicization of liberal education" relies on a patently false assertion. John Agresto, president of St. John's College in New Mexico, claims that radicals deny the possibility of reading texts "nonpolitically" because they deny "transtemporal and universal truths or principles."

NAS has taken credit for the repeal of a University of Michigan speech code—intended to reduce racist and sexist incidents on campus. With support from NAS and the Michigan chapter of the ACLU, Wesley Wynne, a graduate student in biological psychology, sued his alma mater and won. In 1989, a federal court ruled that UM's speech code was so broadly defined as to threaten the First Amendment.

According to a favorable article in the *Chronicle of Higher Education*, NAS now has 1,400 members, statewide affiliates in 17 states and campus chapters at the Universities of Minnesota at Twin Peaks, New Mexico at Albuquerque, Texas at Austin, and at Duke and Emory Universities. And NAS has some concrete plans to expand its influence.

In early 1990, all NAS members received a 38-page questionnaire prepared by the affiliated Madison Center, founded in 1988 by Allan Bloom and then-Secretary of Education William Bennett. (In September 1990, the Center merged with the Institute for Educational Affairs, and is now known as the hybrid Madison Center for Educational Affairs.) The survey is an amazingly thorough intelligence-gathering tool. Respondents are asked to provide detailed answers to questions like: How often does the administration play an active role in tenure decisions? What are the prevailing attitudes toward ROTC and CIA recruitment on campus? How conspicuous is the homosexual faculty presence on campus?

Some of the data is liable to find its way into "The Madison Guide: A Commonsense Scorecard on America's Colleges," scheduled for publication in 1991. The guide will focus on "how education and teaching has fared under the mixed influences of the last 15 or 20 years," says Madison Center V.P. Charles Horner, a former State Department, U.S. Information Agency, and RAND Corporation official.

NAS has set up a Research Center in Princeton—consistent with the 1984 Richardson plan—to "accumulate information on the issues and trends of contemporary higher education." In its Fall 1990 newsletter, NAS appealed to its members to send in course descriptions and proposals, departmental newsletters, and the like, for trend analysis to be conducted by NAS Research Director Glenn Ricketts.

The survey data from the Madison Center will come in handy as NAS implements a couple of its other plans. One is the new Faculty and Executive Search Service, which is a mini-employment service provided free to NAS members. Another strategy is the formation of caucuses within the professional associations organized by various academic disciplines. Already, NAS and the Intercollegiate Studies Institute have formed anti-liberal groupings within the Modern Language Association, the American Historical Association, and the American Philosophical Association, according to ISI National Director Chris Long.

A November 1990 mailing to the Sociology-Anthropology section of NAS, from Dan McMurry of Middle Tennessee State University, spelled out an effort to "reform from within" the American Sociological Association. Hardly a hotbed of radicalism, the ASA exists to promote the careers of its members, who are mostly mild-mannered theorists more interested in studying the world than changing it. NAS plans to begin sponsoring special sessions at ASA meetings. How convenient—the current president of the ASA is University of Chicago Professor James S. Coleman, a prominent member of NAS. The "Dear Colleague" letter warned NAS members to "avoid being regarded as conservative. We hope to cast our nets widely."

Knowledge is Power

NAS will succeed if and only if progressives don't do their homework. The first step is for people to learn the nature of the right-wing game plan on their own campuses. Who are the administrators and faculty out to block proposals and hirings that would improve university teaching and research? Which faculty are vulnerable to attack from the Right and how might they be supported? Are their opponents motivated by misguided notions of what academic pluralism should mean, or are they part of an NAS chapter or something like it? In what ways are rightist faculty mobilizing students to do their bidding? The right-wing student groups that have harassed liberal professors are often the same ones involved in racist and sexist attacks on other students, and in infiltration of the student Left.

An energetic analysis and discussion of the Right's intellectual arguments is as important as knowing the political line-up on campus. Just as the Smith-Richardson Foundation advocated "high-ground articulation," so should the Left take the initiative in debates around important questions for which there are no easy answers. Should degree programs include a core curriculum, including specific sets of books which simply must be mastered by everyone within the discipline? Do punitive sanctions for users of "fighting words" on campus *really* reduce racist and sexist violence, or are such measures misguided infringements on free speech that might *also* have the effect of exacerbating conflict? The Left ought not to find itself in a position of taking knee-jerk positions that seem "politically correct" or expedient in a short term sense. Rather, the campus Left should develop a deserved reputation as the group of people most open to rational, democratic decisionmaking, even if that means taking positions—for principled reasons—that are also voiced by some conservatives.

To do otherwise might mean surrendering education as one more institution committed to the preservation of the powers that be.

Notes on
Political Correctness

Z Magazine, July/August 1993

Two years ago, readers could not have escaped the daily newspapers' barrage of op-ed page warnings on the scourge of "political correctness." From Ivy League to community colleges— so the storytellers claimed—leftists, radical feminists and angry people of color had seized the wheels of higher education. The fate of Western Civilization hung in the balance. D'Nesh D'Souza became an overnight success with his *Illiberal Education*, a grab bag of anecdotes about campus zealotry. Leading the anti-PC charge was the National Association of Scholars (NAS), the Right's first sustained organization of university faculty nationwide.

Progressive intellectuals began to fight back, namely by exposing the PC hunters' decidedly political agenda and by grappling rationally with PC-related campus issues like speech codes and multicultural curriculum requirements. Gerald Graff's group Teachers for a Democratic Culture and Stanley Aronowitz's Union of Democratic Intellectuals have sought to open lines of communication among people concerned with true academic freedom—and the threat posed to it by the Right.

It was only a matter of time before the PC scare stories would lose their power to interest—let alone alarm—the larger public and the editors of the mainstream press. The mass propaganda campaign against "political correctness," like other moral panics of the Reagan-Bush era, has filtered into the memory banks of what we call "conventional wisdom."

One by-product of the "political correctness" campaign was the National Association of Scholars' consolidation of a network of 3,000 faculty members, organized into 29 state affiliates. Gracing the NAS advisory board is an array of prominent neoconservative intellectuals, including Jeane Kirkpatrick, Irving Kristol, Seymour Martin Lipset and John Bunzel. The membership itself spans the range of high-status private universities to small community colleges. It cost NAS a bundle in promotional work to recruit each member, and that would not have been possible without NAS' bottomless pit of corporate foundation grants. But a handful of well-coordinated NAS members on any given campus can make a big difference during hiring and curriculum battles. Recently NAS members at the University of New Mexico came to the aid of a part-time instructor charged with using racist rhetoric. At the University of Minnesota, two NAS professors used the campus newspaper to "expose" a supposedly rough-handed sexual harassment training session required for liberal arts faculty. Three years ago, NAS made a national splash when its University of Texas affiliate succeeded in blocking an English department proposal to supplement readings for a composition course with a sociology textbook on race and gender issues.

The National Association of Scholars Conference

Aware of the association's limited local successes and its polemicists' larger role in the anti-PC campaign, I signed up to attend NAS' fourth national convention, held this April at San Francisco's Park Lane Parc Fifty-Five Hotel. The event offered no major surprises, but it was a good chance to hear NAS members' viewpoints. Naturally, I was one of only about two dozen women present among 250 registrants, virtually all of them middle-aged and white, except for two invited black speakers. But, then, how "politically correct" of me to have noticed.

NAS President Stephen Balch opened the conference with a call for members to recognize their accomplishments in making "political correctness" a household term. He urged them to prepare for a "protracted journey toward higher education reform" and to move from a critique of PC to "building institutions" and finding ways to wield political influence via conservative alumni and state legislators.

From there, the first panel was scheduled to take on one of the most important questions facing anyone concerned about an educated citizenry: "Can Higher Education be Mass Education?" First up was Jeffrey Hart, professor of English at Dartmouth College and a former, long-time editor of William F. Buckley's

National Review. Hart pulled no punches. Because inherent intelligence capabilities are distributed unevenly along a bell-shaped curve, what proportion of the population, he asked, can go on to universities without making a joke of the adjective 'higher?' Hart's crude elitism won over the NAS audience. He stressed the frivolity of gearing academic standards to people better off relegated to blue collar destinies. "I'd just as soon the fellow fixing my auto brakes is not at the same time pondering *Finnegan's Wake*," he chuckled.

Next to speak was Barry Munitz, Chancellor of the 20-campus California State University system, who thought it would be a dandy idea if his auto mechanic might also be thinking about great works of literature. Munitz' curriculum vitae impressed the California legislators who hired him two years ago to make the financially strapped Cal State system function like a for-profit corporation. Munitz was vice chair of Pacific Lumber's parent corporation, Maxxam Inc., responsible for raiding parts of California's forests. Formerly chancellor of the University of Houston, Munitz also sat on the board of one of Texas' failed savings and loans.

As a bottom line kind of a guy, Munitz emphasized the demographics of California's changing student population. Between 1970 and the projections for the year 2020, California's kindergarten through high school population will have grown from 4.5 million to 10.5 million students. Among these, the percentage of Anglos will have dropped from 74 percent to 25 percent; the percentage of African Americans will have remained constant; Asians will have jumped from two to 19 percent of the total; and the percentage of Hispanic students will have grown from 15 to 48 percent. Munitz was later taken to task by NAS members for his mere acknowledgement of California's changing ethnic make-up. But his point was to stress that, ethnicity aside, California's so-called "master plan" for higher education remains valid. The state pledged several decades ago to make an affordable college education available to every California resident. The top eighth of high school students are supposed to be able to attend the University of California, the top third a Cal State University campus, and the top two thirds a community college of their choice. Munitz offered no clue as to how the state can maintain such access when spiralling fees are driving students away in droves. But he said there are "life and death matters" at stake in California's current educational crisis. "What happens to the economy of California and the United States if we don't try to take a large number of young people and make them better?"

Munitz' speech was not exactly music to the NAS members' ears. After the first panel, they lined up, one after another, to blast Munitz and the last speaker, Robert Rosenzweig from the Association of American Universities, for not indicting fellow college administrators, particularly over affirmative action in hiring and admissions. NAS treasurer Barry Gross summed up the prevailing sentiment that vocational schools are the proper destination for working class high school graduates. To send them into the universities is to lower the standards for those who *really* belong there. Jeffrey Hart said it best: "The broadening of the student body has led to a corruption of the curriculum."

This blatant elitism, of course, contradicted another theme prevalent throughout the NAS conference. These people seem to actually believe that leftist intellectuals constitute a "cultural elite" now in charge of most social science and humanities departments.

After lunch the first day of the conference, keynote speaker and UCLA public policy professor James Q. Wilson explained that today's "threat to academic freedom" comes from within the universities themselves. That's why the media and the general public hardly know there's a problem. Academia has previously endured the dangers of Marxism, Wilson said. "But at least Marxists had a coherent theory. Marxism as a pseudoscience has not survived, but the Marxist animus against bourgeois culture has endured, and like a vampire it can assume many forms." Masquerading, especially in the humanities, under cover of postmodernism, deconstructionism, and other brands of esoterica, these new "vampires" make old-fashioned Marxists look like the Sunday choir. "The university has always had leftists, but never before like the ones we have now," Wilson warned. "These new leftists rebel against *reason*, not just against institutions."

In his nostalgic preference for old-fashioned Marxists over their new postmodern cousins, of course, Wilson conveniently glossed over the history of academic institutions, never a hospitable place for active leftists. The McCarthy era purges were welcomed by the neoconservatives' 1950s forerunners, most explicitly by Sidney Hook, in whose memory the National Association of Scholars grants an annual award. (This year's Sidney Hook Memorial Award was accepted by liberal Yale historian C. Vann Woodward.)

Professor Gerald Early entertained the NAS crowd by reminding them that they should be thankful that a sympathetic scholar like himself now runs the African and Afro-American Studies department at Washington University in St. Louis. A few members of NAS' sociology subsection balked when Early blamed radical sociologists of the early 1960s for spawning what he considers to be dubious new fields like women's and ethnic studies. (Scholars committed to "reason" and "truth" at least ought to get their facts straight.)

A Blast From the Past

In an effort to dispel its neoconservative reputation, NAS balanced its panels with a politically correct number of token liberals. U.C. Berkeley sociology Professor Todd Gitlin joined a panel on "The Mission of the University: Intellectual Discovery or Social Transformation?" For this scene, Gitlin was cast as the kind of leftist an NAS member could agree to disagree with. But Gitlin's presence proved too much for fellow Sixties veteran David Horowitz, who rose from the crowd to attack Gitlin as an unrepentant "apologist" for the Left. Gitlin denied the charge and called Horowitz a few choice names, while NAS President Stephen Balch tried to restore gentlemanly decorum.

Unofficially, some NAS members object to Horowitz' militant theatrics and the yellow journalism of the new tabloid he and Peter Collier mass produce, *Heterodoxy*. In a recent letter-to-the-editor, NAS member Alan Kors of the University of Pennsylvania took *Heterodoxy* to task for the "anti-intellectualism" of its "obsession with gay and lesbian issues." In lock-step with the rest of the Right, Horowitz and Collier have taken to queer-baiting in almost every issue. They answered Kors' letter to the effect that they don't object to garden variety gays and lesbians. "Our issue," they write, "is with the homosexual Left, often self-identified as the Queer Left, which has an agenda that is socially destructive and intellectually fascistic." To drive home the gay-red connection, a *Heterodoxy* cover story on "Queer Studies" dressed a cartoon of Karl Marx in a steel mesh bra, garter belt, stockings and high heels, with a vibrator in one hand and a whip in the other. Pretty sophisticated stuff.

But no one can argue with *Heterodoxy* as an attention grabber. Publicity hounds Horowitz and Collier were featured in a recent promotional article for *Heterodoxy* in the *San Francisco Chronicle*. The supposedly respectable *Chronicle of Higher Education* did its own puff piece on the latest venture of the "two disillusioned radicals," and solicited comments from friends and detractors. NAS president Stephen Balch praised *Heterodoxy* for its "rock-em, sock-em commentary" and "investigative journalism."

Horowitz and Collier call their work a "samizdat publication inside the gulag of the PC university." *Heterodoxy* is really the latest meal ticket for Horowitz and Collier to feed from the same corporate foundation troughs that sustain NAS and a host of right-wing think tanks. Through his Los Angeles-based Center for the Study of Popular Culture—funded by the Olin, Bradley, Scaife and other foundations to the tune of about $700,000 a year— Horowitz has purchased mailing lists to mail as many as 80,000 free copies of each issue of *Heterodoxy*. With only about 8,000 paid subscribers, *Heterodoxy* depends on the same right-wing funders who, in the mid-1980s, launched Horowitz and Collier on a series of "Second Thoughts" conferences, where the two "former radicals" rehearsed their political conversion stories, like a pair of missionaries sent from on high.

Heterodoxy is a forum for its editors to keep fighting old enemies from the Sixties and to establish themselves as arbiters of the Right's current preoccupations. Under the title "Alien Nation: the Illegal Lobby," *Heterodoxy* contributor K.L. Billingsley promotes anxiety about "illegal aliens" from Mexico. "Civic structures are rupturing under the load, school curricula are being changed, prisons and hospitals are becoming inadvertent Ellis Islands, and an ecosystem of crime has sprung up around these immigrants." Why can't the INS patrol the borders, Billingsley asks. "The short answer is that there is a powerful lobby for illegal immigration, a network of organizations that includes the Mexican American Legal Defense and Education Fund (MALDEF), the Latino Issues Forum, the National Council of La Raza, the Coalition for Immigrant and Refugee Rights and Services, etc." What these organizations have to do with academic "political correctness" is anyone's guess.

But *Heterodoxy*'s obsession with "criminals" and sexual deviance suggests a method to the apparent madness of the hunt for "political correctness." Neoconservative social scientists— including a few now at home within the National Association of Scholars— have built careers explaining social movements they don't like as the domain of irrational paranoids who just won't play by the rules of "democracy." One of the neoconservatives' intellectual accomplishments was to build theories that obscured the rational motives driving social movements. These theories, first generated in application to the "radical right" (an oxymoron), were later deployed against the New Left. The current neoconservative attack on feminists and multiculturalists works by perpetuating caricatures of slightly demented zealots, hungry for power.

It might be tempting to see the PC hunters, likewise, as reacting in a thoroughly paranoid style against unreal threats to their high status in academia. But that would be to deny that the old guard really does have something to worry about. No longer can universities, if they so desire, deny access to women and people of color with impunity. Some academic trendiness is worthy of mockery. Plenty is now also up for debate, though fair debate may be impossible inside institutions never intended to be democratic. In defense of the status quo, right-wing intellectuals resort to the reliable tactic of stigmatizing potential contenders for power and scarce resources. Jobs, publishing venues, status within disciplinary pecking orders—these are like gold for the "politically correct" and "incorrect" alike.

Multicultural educators seek to level the playing field in part by reducing the stigma attacked to social groups traditionally subordinate—if visible at all—in privileged places like universities. If the point of the PC hunters is to restigmatize emergent groups demanding a piece of the pie, it is at the same time to elevate the status of a threatened intellectual elite. The NAS represents a cohort of aging academics who see their colleagues' empty seats being filled by new categories of outsiders, and precisely at a time when the financial squeeze is on.

Fiddling While Rome Burns

What betrays NAS' professed concern with academic "standards" more than anything else is the PC hunters' neglect of the universities' bottom-line crisis. California's crown jewel UC and Cal State campuses are falling apart before our eyes, and the organized defenders of Western Civilization are busy counting how many deconstructionists can dance on the head of a pin.

The nation's most populous state can no longer afford to send all its qualified students to college at an affordable rate. No doubt, the situation is similar elsewhere. For the past few years, the state legislature has been reducing funds allocated to the University of California and California State University campuses. In March, the UC Board of Regents voted to raise students' annual fees by 33 percent or $995 yearly, cut enrollment by 2,000 students and eliminate 1,000 jobs. Within the CSU system, fees rose 40 percent, to an average of $1,308, this year, and the state legislature has proposed raising fees by another 37 percent for the coming year. UC Berkeley is planning to cut out more than four percent of its course offerings. Other campuses have already eliminated entire departments.

At some CSU campuses, local corporations have expressed an interest in sponsoring select courses. The dangers are obvious. As they routinely influence state legislators' priorities, corporations are never really out of the loop. But given a direct role within particular universities, they will fund only those programs deemed economically correct. Direct corporate funding may persuade politicians and taxpayers, too, that universities can survive without public money. The job of state legislators is to satisfy their campaign donors, balance budgets, and keep conflicting groups of citizens from voting them out of office. To the extent that universities appear as hotbeds of contentiousness, the politicians can more legitimately reduce their share of funding. Then higher education will surely not be for everyone.

Repentant Radical Rants About PBS

The Guardian, May 29, 1991

Former leftist David Horowitz won't be satisfied until he's put a stop to "the political reconstruction of U.S. history" on the Public Broadcasting System.

But he's not talking about the kind of "reconstruction" that goes on week in and week out on PBS' line-up of right-wing talk shows: William F. Buckley's "Firing Line," the "McLaughlin Group'" "One-on-One," "American Interests," and "Wall Street Week," nor on the nightly "MacNeil-Lehrer News Hour," with its heavy reliance on administration sources.

Horowitz has launched the Committee on Media Integrity (COMINT), he says, not because he has any quarrel with these "talking heads" shows but rather to attack the "legions of panoramic 'documentaries' and 'investigative reports' that attempt to sway audiences in a liberal or radically left direction." Horowitz refers specifically to PBS' recent airing of "Framing the Panthers in Black and White," "The Sixties," and a series about the civil rights movement, "Eyes on the Prize."

The Committee consists of a post office box in Hollywood, a short list of advisory board members, a slick newsletter and a mailing list of several thousand. The group is a project of Horowitz's Center for the Study of Popular Culture, registered as a foundation in order to accept tax-deductible donations.

Thus far, COMINT's claim to fame has been its role in stigmatizing "South Africa Now," the award-winning weekly news show produced by Global Vision. For lack of funding, the show will go off the air. But before money was the determining factor, Horowitz took credit last fall when two PBS stations (KCET in Los Angeles and WGBH in Boston) temporarily canceled the show.

Horowitz, who claims "South Africa Now" was biased in favor of the African National Congress, boasts that he mounted no public pressure campaign to get the program off the air. He merely "applied the powers of persuasion," in several private conversations with KCET station manager Stephen Kulczycki. Managers at both stations promptly reversed their decisions in the face of vocal opposition from viewers. In the case of KCET, says "South Africa Now" producer Danny Schecter, "their own community board and half their staff joined the community to protest."

But Horowitz won a partial victory in that KCET reinstated the program only after tagging each broadcast with a "Point of View" label. Schecter says this "scarlet letter" distinguishes a station disclaimer. "This is a function of PBS' attempt to appease the Horowitzes of this world, who have no constituency and no base," says Schecter.

Horowitz was not appeased. In December COMINT formally petitioned the Federal Communications Commission (FCC) not to renew KCET's broadcast license. Under FCC rules, anyone can file such a petition. More often than not, such challenges are not taken seriously, but instead function as a publicity tactic. Horowitz told the *Los Angeles Times* that he will withdraw his petition as soon as the station establishes an elected board of directors, which some PBS stations already have.

The Radical Specter

Horowitz's presumed credibility as a media critic rests largely on his status as a repentant radical. Once considered a leading New Left intellectual, Horowitz co-authored with Peter Collier several historical books, including a bestseller on the Rockefeller dynasty. In the early 1970s Horowitz edited *Ramparts* magazine and helped organize the Black Panther Party-sponsored East Oakland Community School.

According to a 1987 *Mother Jones* profile of Horowitz, it was the 1974 murder of Ramparts bookkeeper Betty Van Patter—later attributed to one or more Panthers—that propelled him into a spiral of disillusionment and resentment, first toward the Panthers, but eventually toward the entire Left.

By the 1980s, Horowitz and Collier burned their bridges behind them by publishing "Lefties for Reagan" in the

Washington Post Magazine. The utility of the "former leftist" theme was not lost on conservative opinion shapers. Soon after the publication of the *Washington Post* article, Horowitz says, he and Collier were contacted by James Denton of the National Forum Foundation, one of the best-financed of the Right's Washington, D.C., think tanks. The foundation became Horowitz and Collier's East Coast headquarters. Denton, who is the son of the former Alabama Senator Jeremiah Denton, netted hundreds of thousands of corporate foundation dollars for the two ex-radicals to do ideological battle with the Left.

Beginning in 1987, the foundation sponsored a series of widely publicized "Second Thoughts" conferences, at which panels of middle-aged "former leftists" denounced the anti-war and civil rights movements and, more generally, something they call "left culture." The Second Thoughts forums coincided with corporate media's interest, from about 1987 to 1990, in sensationalizing, if not rewriting the history of 1960s activism. Left interpretations of the anti-war and civil rights movements could be "balanced" if not upstaged by those of the ostensibly more thoughtful "radicals" who'd finally come to their senses.

In 1989, Simon and Schuster published Horowitz and Collier's book *Destructive Generation*, an "exposé" of the '60s Left, which met rave reviews from the *Washington Post, Wall Street Journal,* and *Business Week.* (The book's treatment of FBI covert operations against the Black Panthers is instructive. COINTELPRO is mentioned twice and only in passing references, for the purpose of diminishing its historical significance.)

One of the insidious ideological elements of the Second Thoughts Project was the linking of NFF's stable of "ex-leftists" with high-ranking "former Sandinistas," some of whom were by 1987 on the Contra payroll as they shared the podium with Horowitz and Company. In 1987 Horowitz and Collier toured Nicaragua courtesy of the U.S. Information Agency, and returned to tell the requisite Sandinista atrocity stories.

Recently, as peace activists mobilized against the Persian Gulf war, Horowitz again capitalized on his "former radical" persona, with a speech before the American Bar Association's Law and National Security Committee, and with articles in a number of right-wing magazines. He warned that "the organized opposition to America's role in the Gulf that manifests itself in coalitions, demonstrations, and 'teach-ins' on college campuses" is really not a peace movement at all. It's a "nihilistic force whose goal is to deconstruct and dismantle America as a democracy and as a nation."

With this kind of rhetoric, Horowitz remains popular on the right-wing lecture circuit, especially at events sponsored by "conservative" student groups. His faded jeans and occasional use of four-letter words help confirm these activists' stereotypes of what "leftists" are like.

Horowitz is adept at tailoring his message to his audience. At the beginning of an hour-long phone interview, he was raucous and agitated, ranting about the "lunatic left" and "fringe elements" dominating PBS programming. Noticing the silence on my end, he asked if I had ever been part of the Left. I reminded him that I'm reporting for the *Guardian*. "The *Guardian*?" he asked. "I thought you were a Moonie."

In his bluster, he had mistaken my words "*New York Guardian*," for "*New York City Tribune*," a Moonie paper, and had proceeded to play what he thought was an appropriate role. "Oh, well, let's start this conversation again," he said, apologetically. So you're part of the looney left." But from that point on, he was cordial, even friendly—as if we were two old chums chatting in some Berkeley cafe.

The Ghosts of His Past

Horowitz's current media project has emerged precisely at a time when the Left has developed effective institutions for media criticism. The Institute for Media Analysis is in the second year of publishing its monthly magazine, *Lies of Our Times*, focusing on distortions in elite print and news media. Fairness and Accuracy in Reporting (FAIR) has produced solid research on the highly imbalanced set of "expert" sources used by ABC's "Nightline," PBS' "MacNeil/Lehrer News Hour," and, during the recent Persian Gulf crisis, network news in general.

Along comes David Horowitz with an exclusive focus on public broadcasting and the claim that his is a "modest goal" of getting PBS documentaries to "reflect Republican values" on an occasional basis. "I'm actually sympathetic to the complaint of the Left, that there's a Buckley show and no weekly show of the Left," he told the *Guardian*. "But what the Left gets all the time is prime time shows that reconstruct whole reality. What the Right gets is talking head shows."

"Only Horowitz has ever advanced an argument that what's more important is documentary," responds FAIR's director Jeff Cohen. But "that regular line-up on PBS is key because when Buckley, et al., want to harangue about an issue, they have the ability to do it. Clearly what's more significant is who has the power to shape the debate when the debate is going on."

Furthermore, says Cohen, while PBS is "one of the few places that once in a while has a progressive documentary," Horowitz simply doesn't have his facts straight. Most of the documentaries aired on PBS stations are neutral or centrist. "Horowitz just wants to deny any media access by the Left," Cohen concludes.

Toward that end, Horowitz has a number of plans. This fall, when PBS is scheduled to rebroadcast its series "The Sixties," Horowitz will shift into high gear with a loud publicity campaign. Currently, he is lobbying PBS stations to air a film on nuclear energy, funded in large part by the Department of Energy. At the same time, he has teamed up with "an independent producer" who's been funded by PBS in the past, to make a documentary which Horowitz will then try to get aired.

When asked about his plans for public radio, Horowitz was quick to blast the Pacifica network—not the more prominent National Public Radio (NPR). One of his goals is to deprive the Pacifica stations of the small proportion of funding they receive from the government's Corporation on Public Broadcasting. Lacking the ability to wage such a campaign himself, he says, he has encouraged Reed Irvine of Accuracy in Media to take up the charge.

Horowitz reserves his greatest energy (and animosity) for Global Vision. The production company has just released the pilot for "Rights and Wrongs," a new weekly series on international human rights issues. Already, many PBS stations have expressed interest in scheduling the show for the fall. Should "Rights and Wrongs" overcome the funding obstacles that led to the termination of "South Africa Now," Horowitz will lobby against it. "I'm going to appeal to people, send letters to Congress, go to the station boards, go to PBS directly, go to CPB, whatever I can," he rails, with amazing intensity.

In the late 1960s, Global Vision's executive producer Danny Schecter worked for Horowitiz as a *Ramparts* reporter. Now, says Schecter, Horowitz "seems to be spending an inordinate amount of time targeting many of the people who helped with an earlier part of his career. David Horowitz seems to have a personal pathological obsession with the ghosts of his own past."

Personal or not, pathological or not, Horowitz's COMINT provides PBS managers with a convenient come-back when they hear from progressive groups seeking better representation on "public" television. They're getting flack from "both sides," so they must be doing something right.

Project Rand

Written with Richard Hatch

Z Magazine, May 1991

Behind all those "smart bombs" used to crush bridges and water purification facilities, behind all those facts and figures about Iraqi weapons arsenals, the prevailing price of oil, and the strategic advantages of violence over diplomacy, sits a storehouse of brain power that makes modern warfare possible. Central to the planning of the war on Iraq, and a myriad of other U.S. misadventures over the past 45 years, has been the RAND Corporation, appropriately the first federally funded policy-planning outfit to inspire the term "think tank."

RAND (short for research and development) was founded in 1946, as a joint project of the Air Force and Douglas Aircraft, and remained dependent on War Department contracts after it was separately incorporated in 1948. In the aftermath of the United States' first use of nuclear weapons, RAND was a place where the strategic geniuses of the 1950s could put their heads together to construct the kind of mass killing capability that would insure U.S. supremacy into the 21st century. RAND was where men like Bernard Brodie, Herman Kahn and Albert Wohlstetter weighed "kill probabilities" and dreamed of "anticipatory counterattacks" against "urban-industrial targets," otherwise known as cities. It was where Wohlstetter developed the "delicate balance of terror" as the guiding doctrine of the nuclear arms race between the U.S. and the Soviet Union.

With headquarters in sunny Santa Monica, RAND is conveniently close to some of California's best universities (from which it recruits) and to the lucrative military corporations that help line its coffers. Over the years, RAND's size and scope has grown steadily. Its current annual budget of more than $90 million enables RAND to staff departments outside of its primarily military mandate, in areas as seemingly unrelated as judicial reform, drug policy, teacher-training, and health care. RAND's major grants of over $100,000 come from predictable sources: numerous branches of the Pentagon and CIA, as well as Boeing, Citicorp, Exxon, IBM, Xerox, and the like. An indication of RAND's clout is the fact that in one year alone, RAND experts testified before Congress 17 times.

Among both private think tanks and public agencies, RAND distinguishes itself as the operator of three out of three dozen special sites known as "Federally Funded Research and Development Centers" (FFRDCs). At RAND, these include Project Air Force, the U.S. Army's Arroyo Center, and the National Defense Research Institute, operated by the Office of the Secretary of Defense. RAND's prominence among FFRDCs is significant because, according to a 1986 Congressional Research Service Report, "Science Support by the Department of Defense," only a handful of the FFRDCs provide the Department of Defense (DoD) with "objective sources of analysis, evaluation, and advice on general and specific problems of national security."

Beyond the DoD's institutional reliance on RAND, there's the revolving door nature of personnel transfers between RAND and the Pentagon. Through that door marched Donald Rice, who after 17 years as RAND President joined the Bush administration as Secretary of the Air Force. Back at RAND, Rice was replaced by Project Air Force V.P. James A. Thomson.

It was on behalf of the DoD, between 1964 and 1968, that RAND conducted more than 2,000 interviews with North Vietnamese and Viet Cong prisoners and defectors. The resulting 62,000 pages of interview transcripts—kept secret from the U.S. public until 1971—provided the Pentagon with the most detailed intelligence profile available on the "enemy." But according to a 1972 *Ramparts* magazine expose, RAND project head Leon Goure distorted his summary analyses so as to cater to the Johnson administration's wishful thinking about the weaknesses of the Vietnamese resistance. By encouraging Johnson's "light-at-the end-of-the-tunnel" mentality, RAND helped justify the escalation of the U.S. air and ground war after 1965, thereby facilitating the annihilation of countless more Southeast Asian people and helping raise the death toll for U.S. GIs, to boot.

RAND drew public attention when the *New York Times*, in 1971, published former RAND employee Daniel Ellsberg's photocopied set of the "Pentagon Papers," documenting a pattern of government lying about the U.S. role in Vietnam. Since the early 1970s, however, anti-war activists have neglected to scrutinize the fruits of RAND's intellectual pursuits, though RAND remains central to the policymaking process. What follows is a survey of some of RAND's bright ideas.

Pro and Contra

The extensive Viet Cong Motivation and Morale Project established RAND's credentials in the field of counterinsurgency, which by the 1980s was euphemistically termed "low intensity conflict." In practice, LIC strategy includes the selective use of political, military and economic pressures in three types of scenarios: against standing governments deemed inimical to U.S. interests; against armed revolutionary movements contesting the power of U.S. allies; and, preemptively, against progressive peasant and labor unions, churches, student and environmental groups. RAND has contributed to LIC strategy for all three contingencies around the globe.

During the U.S. war in Southeast Asia, RAND trained U.S. counterinsurgency operatives at the Naval Reserves Officers School in Long Beach, California, and conducted dozens of classified and public studies on tactics from aerial bombardment to supply-line interdiction to "night pacification patrolling."

In 1987, RAND contracted with the DoD to figure out why, in late 1985, the U.S. military had not predicted the imminent collapse of Ferdinand Marcos' regime in the Philippines. RAND analyzed both public and private stability assessments, and concluded that U.S. strategists had failed to foresee the impact of short-term factors like Marcos' electoral fraud and the shift of Philippine military leaders' allegiance to Corazón Aquino.

Elsewhere in the Pacific, RAND counterinsurgency expert George Tanham toured the islands of Fiji, Vanuatu, Papua New Guinea and Tonga between 1987 and 1989 for the Office of the Under-Secretary of Defense for Policy. Tanham found trouble in paradise, and reported back on growing "anti-American attitudes" among churches, labor unions and the anti-nuclear movement. Tanham warned of potential Soviet influence and recom-

mended increased U.S. aid, educational exchanges and the circulation of pro-Western videotapes. He also urged continued "assistance" to labor unions, particularly through the Asian-American
Free Labor Institute (AAFLI) which, in fact, gets substantial funding from the National Endowment for Democracy.

In Latin America, RAND's study of emerging political trends
dates back to the 1960s. In 1969 RAND released "The Changing
Catholic Church," one of the earliest forecasts of the political
implications of liberation theology. The report, prepared for State
Department intelligence, detailed the political tendencies of religious leaders in Peru, Colombia, Brazil and Chile. In the case of
Chile, RAND traced the history of the progressive lay Catholic
youth movement Iglesia Joven and pointed ominously to its neme-
sis, the Society for the Defense of Tradition, Family and Property.
A few years later, TFP, as it's commonly known, was one of the
pro-fascist groups used by the CIA to destabilize and overthrow
the elected government of Salvador Allende.

In the late 1970s, RAND terror expert Brian Jenkins, himself
a former Green Beret paratrooper, began advocating that governments threatened by guerrilla movements receive U.S. training in
countersubversive propaganda, interrogation tactics and the
establishment of strategic hamlets. Such methods were tailor-
made for warfare against rebel forces in Guatemala and El
Salvador. As such, in 1982, Jenkins' blueprint was adopted by the
U.S. Special Forces as its own working model for counterinsurgency.

By 1984 Jenkins was also working the pro-insurgency side of
the LIC fence, when he recommended that the U.S. wage proxy
warfare on Nicaragua. As the Contra war continued, Jenkins and
other RAND staffers convened a pair of strategy meetings in
1987 and 1988, attended by high-ranking Contra leaders, U.S.
military and State Department officials.

While the Contras attacked farms, oil depots and other economic targets, RAND economists quietly studied methods to
deprive Nicaragua of much needed international credit. The
Reagan administration blocked loans from the World Bank and
the Inter-American Development Bank, and in 1985 imposed a
full U.S. embargo on Nicaragua. In 1986 RAND economists

under contract to the DoD recommended that the U.S. cut off Nicaragua's access to foreign export credit subsidies. Many developing countries, lacking hard currency and unable to pay commercial interest rates, rely on these subsidies. In a typical arrangement, a relatively well-off nation subsidizes a poorer one by reducing interest rates on loans for the purchase of agricultural supplies, in exchange for a good deal on the harvested export crop. RAND calculated that export credit subsidies to Nicaragua amounted to nearly $200 million between 1981 and 1984, and proposed to U.S. planners that "if European governments are alerted to the costs of providing export credits to Nicaragua, they might reduce these flows, if not to further U.S. policy, perhaps because it is in their interest."

No wonder Nicaraguan leaders faced difficulty obtaining financial assistance from Western European governments as the Contra war dragged on. Had solidarity activists better understood the sources and methods of the economic warfare waged against Nicaragua, we might have more effectively challenged the propaganda theme that the Sandinistas were responsible for the country's economic plight.

A similar economic pressure strategy has been the subject of numerous RAND studies on the economies of the Soviet Union and Eastern Europe. One 1984 RAND report to the DoD suggested that the U.S. manipulate Soviet access to high-tech oil drilling equipment. The Soviets have oil but they have to spend a fortune getting it out of the ground. RAND's reasoning was that a simple embargo of drilling equipment sales might increase the Soviets' political interest in access to Persian Gulf oil. So RAND outlined an alternative plan of subsidizing U.S. sales of oil drilling equipment to encourage the Soviets' long-term interest in their own domestic oil production. At the same time, a RAND report noted, proposed one-time access fees on high-tech machinery would deprive Soviet planners of capital they might otherwise channel into military production.

The logic behind such a plan is indicative of how RAND thinks. Consistently, in RAND's position papers, the most cynical brand of cold-blooded pragmatism outrules predictable right-wing ideological preferences.

RAND's work on Ethiopia is a case in point. In 1985 RAND's Africa "scholar" Paul Henze, a former CIA Station Chief based in Ethiopia, recommended against U.S. support for "freedom fighters" arrayed against the central government. Instead Henze suggested that a promise of U.S. military and economic aid to Ethiopia could cause the avowedly Marxist regime to distance itself from the Soviet Union. Henze's position deviated noticeably from that of more strident right-wing activists who never met a band of "freedom fighters" they didn't love.

In a similarly pragmatic vein, in 1989, RAND released a report urging both Israel and the United States to accept the "inevitable compromise" of a Palestinian state as the best option for protecting Israeli "security." The report's author, Graham Fuller, was Vice-Chair of the CIA's National Intelligence Council under the Reagan administration. In a recent interview, Fuller maintained his support for a two-state solution, though, he said, that's unlikely under the current Israeli government.

RAND's Terrorists

In their book *The 'Terrorism' Industry*, Gerry O'Sullivan and Edward Herman rate RAND personnel as leading promoters of the kind of sensationalized view of "terrorists" that justifies any means used against them.

One of the most widely cited terrorologists is RAND's own counterinsurgency advocate Brian Jenkins. He currently divides his time between RAND, where he works on government contracts, and the Los Angeles office of Kroll Associates, a private intelligence firm that helps corporate clients solve petty capitalist crimes like hostile takeovers and computer sabotage.

In a 1985 booklet, "International Terrorism: The Other World War," Jenkins defined his subject broadly: "Terrorism is the use of criminal violence to force a government to change its course of action, usually to withdraw from or desist from undertaking something." Thus follows RAND's ability to deflect scrutiny from what Herman and O'Sullivan term "wholesale," or state-sponsored terrorism practiced routinely by U.S. allies, to the "retail" terrorism of small sects and splinter groups with no official headquarters. Thus follows the terrorologists' fascination with Germany's Bader Meinhof Gang, the Italian Red Brigades and other cliques of exotic conspirators.

Outside of public pronouncements on TV, RAND experts acknowledge that much, if not most, real terror is perpetrated by the Right. In one 1986 study, RAND's Bruce Hoffman expressed surprise that so little attention adheres to the neo-nazi operators who committed "nearly 60 attacks on NATO and American military targets in West Germany."

These types of attacks are not the mainstay of RAND's extensive use of in-house computer databases for terror-analysis. Jenkins has compiled one database of more than 7,000 terrorist incidents. In another project, "Conceptual Frameworks for Analyzing Terrorist Groups" Jenkins and colleagues tested a set of hypotheses on likely terrorist scenarios, by combing "an extensive database on 29 selected terrorist groups" for data on "150 specific attributes" such as "psychology, mindset and decision-making." In another study, project director Bruce Hoffman analyzed the tactics and logistics of 100 "commando raids" conducted by government and miscellaneous "terrorists" between 1946 and 1983 and advised the U.S. Defense Department "that commando warfare and small-group raids may be a useful adjunct to U.S. military policy."

In a June 1985 RAND report, Brian Jenkins advocated that the U.S. use military force in potential terrorist incidents. A few months later, real terrorists hijacked the Italian *Achille Lauro* cruise ship and threw U.S. citizen Leon Klinghoffer overboard. After the hijackers turned themselves in to Egyptian authorities in exchange for safe passage to Algiers, U.S. fighter pilots intercepted an Egyptian airliner carrying the hijackers and forced the plane to land in Sicily where the terrorists could be tried by the Italian government. Jenkins released another report, applauding the Reagan administration's military action but lamenting the "diplomatic disaster" of acting without Egyptian or Italian approval.

Beyond military solutions, RAND advocates rehabilitation of terrorists. One RAND report advises that "terrorists feel alienated from society" and "will probably respond to being taken seriously and respected as individuals." Perhaps that explains why RAND took in Honduran General Gustavo Alvarez Martinez when he was expelled from his country at gunpoint. Alvarez presided over the Honduran army-linked death squads and the Nicaraguan Contras when they were in their formative years. Following Alvarez' ouster in a 1984 barracks coup, the U.S. military promptly dispatched him to RAND, where he landed a position as a consultant on Central America.

While harboring Alvarez—a real terrorist if there ever was one—RAND initiated surveillance of potential "terrorists" in the U.S. anti-nuclear and anti-intervention movements, under contract with the Department of Energy. A 1989 RAND study catalogued more than 170 anti-nuclear and anti-intervention events from San Luis Obispo, California, to Seabrook, New Hampshire, between 1984 and 1987. Each entry details the precise location, date, number of participants, sponsoring organizations, goals and tactics of peaceful protest actions, including teach-ins and vigils. Inexplicably, the supposed "nuclear terrorism" study includes data on demonstrations against apartheid and U.S. intervention in Central America. Though the study's author, Elizabeth Ondaatje, acknowledged that "radical anti-abortionists were responsible for more terrorist activity in the United States in 1985 and 1986 than any other terrorist groups," RAND has yet to publish a single study on violence from the anti-abortion movement.

On the Drawing Board

One of George Bush's closest confidants during the war on Iraq was his National Security Adviser (and fishing partner) Brent Scowcroft, a RAND trustee from 1984 to 1989. According to *New Republic* editor Fred Barnes, it was Scowcroft who encouraged Bush to promote the catch phrase "new world order."

Beyond rhetorical flourish, RAND personnel were among the intellectual authors of the Persian Gulf war. In a pair of DoD-funded conferences in 1985 and 1986, foreign policy experts met at RAND to lay the theoretical groundwork for the use of "cooperative forces." This strategic doctrine, likely to be the United States' working model for the 1990s, begins where the LIC-derived use of foreign nationals leaves off. "Cooperative forces" strategy is intended specifically for scenarios where the combined use of economic pressures, support for local armies, "diplomacy" via agencies like NED and the U.S. Information Agency, and even direct U.S. military action remain ineffective for obtaining "regional security."

As spelled out in RAND conference papers, "cooperative forces," also known as "coalition defense" involves the creation of a division of labor between the militaries of the U.S., its acquiescent First World allies and self-motivated regional elites in the Third World. "Cooperative forces" is more multi-lateral than LIC and is specifically intended to maximize the United States' military resources—increasingly spread thin—while diminishing "public attention and pressure" on the home front.

RAND literally wrote the book on applications of "cooperative forces" strategy. *Developing Cooperative Forces in the Third World*, edited by Charles Wolf, Jr., and Katherine Watkins Webb of RAND, and published in 1987 by Lexington Books, is a collection of the 1985 and 1986 conference papers, worth scrutiny by peace activists.

One of the hypothetical scenarios considered is particularly ominous. In this RAND fantasy, Peru's Shining Path guerrilla movement is taken over by opposing "Cuba-backed rebels," and the Peruvian government calls Uncle Sam for help. The U.S. then provides military hardware and air reconnaissance but enlists Venezuela and Argentina to provide the actual foot soldiers, thus reducing diplomatic problems within Latin America and ensuring small numbers of U.S. body bags.

(A separate March 1985 RAND study, analyzing domestic public opinion data from both the Vietnam and Korean war eras, reported "a strong inverse relationship" between public support for war and the number and duration of casualties, irrespective of U.S. political objectives. RAND, therefore, recommended that "minimizing U.S. casualties should be a central objective in the formulation of new strategies, force configurations and weapon systems for limited war contingencies.")

Far from an insignificant group of intellectuals, the RAND "Cooperative Forces" thinkers included Fred Ikle, then-Under Secretary of Defense; Henry Rowen, former chair of the CIA's National Intelligence Council; and John Norton Moore who, as Counselor on International Law to the Department of State, defended U.S. aggression against Nicaragua in the World Court. (*Developing Cooperative Forces* includes the full conference participants list.)

At the RAND meetings, one of the strongest advocates of "cooperative forces" was Dennis Ross, then-Special Assistant to President Reagan on the National Security Council, and an expert on Arab-Israeli affairs. In 1989 Ross went on to become head of the State Department's Policy Planning Bureau under the Bush administration.

But as early as the 1985 and 1986 RAND meetings, Ross presciently detailed potential war scenarios for the Middle East. He referred to an earlier event, "the Saudis turn to us in the fall of 1980, when they feared the Iran-Iraq war would spread and threaten oil facilities." He suggested that "we need to think about the other factors—that is, legitimizing, economic, and legacy factors—that may either give other states a reason to act or can be used by us to give them a reason to do so." Ross suggested drafting Britain and France as military assets. He noted that the internal political dynamics of Germany and Japan would impede those two heavyweights from deploying their own military forces, and would, instead, consign them to a supportive financial role. Ross lamented the United State's past inability to acquire basing rights in the Middle East and to draw Turkey and other NATO allies into a Persian Gulf military coalition. Another conference participant, RAND consultant James Digby, proposed an even more specific Persian Gulf scenario in which "Iraqi irregulars seize part of Kuwait. At GCC [Gulf Cooperation Council] request, Egypt and Pakistan provide a force to repel them with support from the Saudis and United States."

Sound familiar? It was precisely this caliber of contingency planning that enabled the Bush administration to deploy the U.S. military within days after Iraq did invade Kuwait in August 1990.

While virtually no one outside high-level policymaking circles was looking, RAND was an important venue for some of the official plotting and scheming that made the Persian Gulf war possible, if not pre-ordained. What might be next on the agenda?

After the Storm

Z Magazine, September 1991

The Bush administration is getting mixed reviews for its performance in the New World Order. Months after the United States' supposed victory in the Persian Gulf, right-wing analysts have been slow to frame their post-war debate. But with few exceptions, triumphalist sentiment has been in short supply. In part, that's because all partisans—those who supported the massive killing of Iraqis and those who didn't—know two things: first, that the swift "victory" looked too much like a massacre, and second, that a vigorous controversy over the war's causes and effects could further tear at the Right's crumbling facade of unity in the aftermath of the "Reagan revolution."

Nevertheless, a diversity of viewpoints has emerged in right-wing publications. These viewpoints tend to fall into two categories which I'll call, for the sake of argument, the Quagmire thesis and the Opportunity thesis. The debate between the two camps is more about means than ends, with both sides defining the U.S. "national interest" in terms of economic supremacy and the ability to dictate who allies with whom throughout the world.

The Quagmirists are, generally, more concerned with long-term effects. They argue that the war has been too costly, both because the net bill will further bloat the domestic deficit and, internationally, because the war helped protect oil resources for Japanese and German competitors while sowing seeds of violent Middle Eastern insurgencies which only the U.S. military will be able to contain. The Opportunists look more to the war's short-term benefits: ally Israel's nearby enemies have been temporarily disoriented; the U.S. military got a quick dose of good public relations that will help it weather pending budget cuts; and the Democrats can be made to look even wimpier than usual in time for the 1992 elections.

Apocalypse, Not Yet

Pat Buchanan has been the most vocal proponent of the

Quagmire thesis. From the onset of Iraq's occupation of Kuwait, Buchanan sounded the alarm against U.S. military action in the Persian Gulf. So vociferous were Buchanan's claims last year that only the "Israeli lobby" stood to gain from a Middle East war, that his own record of professional anti-Semitism sparked a verbal duel between so-called "neoconservative" and "paleoconservative" antagonists on the Right.

Predictably, once all bets were off, Buchanan fell quickly in line with his Commander-in-Chief. Writing in the January 25, 1991, issue of his "From the Right" newsletter, Buchanan lauded the performance of the Stealth fighters, Tomahawk and Patriot missiles. "It was natural and the right thing to do, when the guns started, to support U.S. armed forces until victory is attained," he argued in a perverse bit of authoritarian logic. "But when this war ends, we ought to be first to sound the 'All clear!' to reopen the debate over just where America is headed. For with U.S. troops now in Israel manning the Patriots, and a vast U.S. army in the Gulf, we are acquiring permanent commitments in the most explosive region on earth. We don't need any new commitments. We have too many old ones right now."

By June Buchanan was shedding crocodile tears for the victims of U.S. aggression, citing the toll in his insider newsletter: "Hundreds of thousands of Iraqis, soldiers and civilians, Kurds, Shi'ites and Sunnis, are dead; perhaps one million children are fatherless; several million Arab and Asian people are refugees; Iraq is in ruins; Kuwait's oil fields still burn; the Gulf has suffered immense environmental damage, and, according to one study, if the U.S.-led embargo continues, 170,000 more Iraqi children may perish."

Such compassion from a man who, throughout the 1980s, apparently lost little sleep while his precious "freedom fighters" cut off the ears, gouged out the eyes, and slit the throats of countless children in Mozambique, Angola, Nicaragua, Guatemala and El Salvador. Buchanan now worries that the Middle Eastern orphans of the New World Order will grow up to be tomorrow's "terrorists." "Those to whom evil is done do evil in return," he wrote in an April *Washington Times* column. "This thing has quagmire written all over it."

Buchanan's current indignation over U.S.-instigated atrocities might have something to do with his own possible run for the presidency in 1992—a number of right-wing activists are quietly talking about drafting him. These "conservatives" are part of a growing alliance that opposes government intervention in the economy while favoring state enforcement of "traditional family values."

Some among this contradictory "libertarian-moralist" tendency came together against U.S. war plans last fall to form the Committee to Avert a Mideast Holocaust. Before, during and since the war, the Committee has had little public visibility, other than a handful of press releases and a few write-ups in the *Washington Times* and *Human Events* newspapers.

Committee chair Philip Nicolaides says that unlike pro-war groups, his organization has had a difficult time fundraising. Hardly an outsider, Nicolaides is a former deputy director of the Voice of America, which broadcasts pro-U.S. news around the world over shortwave radio. In a telephone interview Nicolaides articulated some of the essentials of the Quagmire thesis: "Israel's survival requires some accommodation with the Arabs," he said. Should Israel, with U.S. backing, continue to stonewall on negotiating with the Palestinians, then "the next time anyone fires missiles at Israel, they'll be more accurate than the Scuds and they'll cause more damage." Among other consequences of such a scenario, Nicolaides foresees a "mass exodus of Israelis." Many might try to emigrate back to the United States.

Concern over a Middle East arms race is valid, and it's being voiced not just by the anti-interventionist camp. In May, *National Review*—whose editors lined up on both sides of the war debate—published Adam Garfinkle's "Will Saddam Get the Bomb?" Garfinkle is a Middle East specialist at the Philadelphia-based Foreign Policy Research Institute, a hawkish think tank if there ever was one. "Hard though it is to fathom," Garfinkle begins, "Saddam and the Ba'ath [party] are still there, they're patient and calculating, and thirst for revenge is not a rare sentiment among Arabs." This "Arabs-are-not-like-us" thesis is an almost axiomatic corollary to the Quagmire thesis. But Garfinkle's main point is that while mutually assured destruction strategy deterred the U.S. and the Soviet Union from annihilating each other, we might not be so lucky if Iraq gets the bomb. "Psychiatrists have characterized Saddam as a malignant narcissist with sociopathic tendencies," Garfinkle writes, finally concluding that deterrence only "works when protector nuclear powers can credibly convince aggressors that aggression will be resisted...." and "no such clarity is possible in the Middle East." Israeli "nuclear protection" of Kuwait and Saudi Arabia would not be a credible threat to Iraq, he argues, nor would any U.S. president credibly order nuclear attacks against Iraq on behalf of Iran, Jordan, or Syria.

In Garfinkle's version of the Quagmire thesis, the world won't be safe until Iraq is permanently disarmed, and that in itself is a dubious prospect.

Long-Range Malignancies

Setting aside the worst case nuclear scenario, right-wing analysts see unending trouble in the Middle East. Thus far, the most elaborate rendition of the Quagmire thesis comes from former *Jerusalem Post* bureau chief Leon T. Hadar, in a policy report released June 12 by the libertarian Cato Institute, where Hadar is an adjunct scholar. Like Garfinkle, Hadar begins his analysis with the requisite "they're-not-like-us" thesis. Unlike the post-World War II "reconstruction of Germany and Japan [which] was successful because it was based on existing and very powerful civil societies, strong national identities, large educated middle classes and previous experience with political and economic freedom," Hadar asserts that "Middle Eastern countries lack the political culture necessary to deal with one of the major dilemmas of politics: how to reconcile order and stability on the one hand and freedom and justice on the other." Because these societies are so culturally backward, so goes this argument, the United States is headed for trouble, even in the best case scenarios.

Having set the obligatory racist framework for discussing Arab politics, Hadar nevertheless proceeds to outline some specific, possible pitfalls the U.S. now faces. "In the long run," he writes, "a radical-fundamentalist regional bloc consisting of Syria, Lebanon, Iraq, and Iran might emerge. Such a bloc would be in a position to control the central region of the Middle East and become a major threat to Israel and the Arab gulf states as well as to any American military presence in the region. That development would create conditions under which Washington could be again asked to prevent aggression and maintain stability." Therefore, Hadar deduces, the United States' most likely move is to try to maintain what he calls a "'user friendly'" version of Saddam: a benign military dictator heading a rival clique inside the ruling Ba'ath party."

Nowhere in the Cato Institute analysis does one find concern for the everyday people who will be living under "benign" military dictatorships, in Iraq or elsewhere. Even from this critic of Bush administration policy, Hadar's projections are based solely on likely effects for U.S. citizens. "Most Americans will be unwilling to accept the proposition that past U.S. policies had something to do with those adverse developments—that an Iraqi kid who lost his parents under the rubble of a Baghdad apartment building destroyed by American bombers might one day hijack an American airliner." The Quagmire thesis means, in part, that U.S. citizens might reap some of the violence sown by their own government. And, as Hadar notes in passing further on in his report, "more Pentagon spending and plans to improve U.S. 'long-reach' military capabilities in the region....would be more politically costly for the United States in terms of support at home."

Lest continuing U.S. intervention in the Middle East exacerbate anti-American blocs there and, ultimately, weaken domestic approval for the U.S. political-economic system, Hadar proposes that the U.S. should now simply let the chips fall where they may. "Washington should consider a new approach: an attitude of neglect toward the Palestinian-Israeli conflict, the kind of attitude it has adopted toward other regional conflicts such as that between India and Pakistan." Forced to fend for themselves, the Israelis might surrender to the negotiation process. But, Hadar concludes, such a policy of benign neglect toward the Arab-Israeli conflict is unlikely because the Gulf War itself strengthened the hand of foreign policymakers most wedded to the military-industrial complex, and most averse to the Cato Institute's preferred emphasis on "international economic competition."

Silver Linings

Counterposed to the pessimistic Quagmirists are the right-wing analysts tallying up opportunities now arising from the Gulf War. Some proponents of the Opportunity thesis see the war's benefits in stark military terms; others are applauding both political and military gains. Those in the latter camp tend to subscribe to the "neoconservative" worldview. These are the erstwhile Cold War liberals who now seem addicted to all forms of U.S. meddling to promote "democracy" and "liberation" near and far.

To date, the most concise neoconservative rendition of the Opportunity thesis comes from *New Republic* editor Fred Barnes, in "Winners and Losers: A Postwar Balance Sheet," found in the Summer 1991 issue of the *National Interest* journal. Barnes outlines six areas in which the "war" was an overall "success." 1) On a world scale, the United States now has more prestige and clout, and "the war makes American military intervention politically easier in the future." 2) In the Middle East, "the security of Israel is now assured for the foreseeable future," because, supposedly, with the defeat of Iraq, "the radical eastern front coalition against Israel no longer exists....Moreover, the PLO is discredited and impoverished," having lost the backing it had from Egypt, Syria, Saudi Arabia and the Gulf states. 3) In Washington, D.C., the power balance within the administration has been tilted away from Secretary of State James Baker—whom Barnes sees as less hawkish than Bush—and more toward Pentagon chief Dick Cheney and General Colin Powell. Perversely, Barnes argues that by virtue of Bush's strongarming of Congress to vote in favor of the war, it's "more likely that future decisions on war will be accompanied by a congressional vote." 4) In the electoral arena, "by opposing the war and arguing lamely that sanctions might have worked, Democrats damaged themselves badly at the presidential level." But Barnes takes solace in his prediction that whatever lack of war fever some Democrats displayed, they're unlikely to suffer severely in 1992 House and Senate races. 5) The press became part of the victory, in part because the Pentagon allowed lots of "live TV coverage from Baghdad and of Scud attacks on Israel" and in part because the "war" ended so swiftly, heading off resentment over the Pentagon pool system. 6) The military scored big, especially with the successful performance of the F-

117 Stealth Fighter. Now, Barnes gushes, stealth technology gives the U.S. heightened ability to wage surprise attacks. "This is as revolutionary a development as the submarine was years ago."

Also rejoicing in the future's "revolutionary" possibilities is Michael Ledeen, the infamous free-lance "terrorism" expert, now ensconced at the American Enterprise Institute. Ledeen played a supporting role in "Irangate" as broker for the three-way deal wherein Israel would ship missiles to Iran which, in turn, would help secure the release of U.S. hostages in Lebanon. In the June 1991 issue of the *American Spectator*, Ledeen claims that Bush pulled a fast one by leading everyone to believe that "the real policy was Smash Saddam," when, in fact, he had every intention of leaving the Kurds and the Shi'ites high and dry. Now, Ledeen proposes, the administration ought to see that corrupt Kuwaiti and Saudi dictators' days are numbered, so the U.S., "the world's one truly revolutionary society," ought to search out every band of "reformers" from Havana to Beijing and help them replace "traditional boundaries" and "traditional leaders."

Ledeen leaves unstated one transparent reality. To the extent that Middle Eastern pots keep boiling, he can continue to sell his consultancy services as a "terrorism consultant" schooled in spy-craft.

Weapons-Think

Military Opportunists are thinking and writing primarily in terms of which weapons systems merit the lion's share of taxpayer support. Budget tightening within the Pentagon is likely to exacerbate normal competition between the various branches of the military. "We will not have the luxury of fielding every developed weapon system," writes Marine Corps Commandant General Alfred M. Gray in the Winter 1991 issue of *Strategic Review*. Naturally, as a Marine, Gray advocates an increased role for "naval expeditionary forces." But other contributors to this journal, published by the U.S. Strategic Institute, argue that since the air war played such a "decisive" role in Desert Storm, air weaponry will be the foundation of U.S. "security" in coming years.

Missiles and anti-missile defense systems are the names of

the game. Writing in the Spring 1991 issue of the Heritage Foundation's *Policy Review*, Angelo Codevilla of the Hoover Institution stresses that the Strategic Defense Initiative (SDI) has been "a welfare program for well-connected scientists....In exchange for eight years and $24 billion, the SDI program has given us not a single usable device." Codevilla blames the SDI production failure on the Reagan and Bush administrations' compliance with the Anti-Ballistic Missile (ABM) Treaty, "which commits us to forgo building a defense on our territory or preparing the base for such a defense." Codevilla calls for the building of "mobile ABM units stationed near cities and moving unpredictably around places that might be targets for missile attacks."

In its own April 18 "Backgrounder" on SDI, the Heritage Foundation cynically attributed the changing political fortunes of high-tech missile defense systems to the Persian Gulf war. "Live TV broadcasts and countless replays of deadly Scud missiles screeching over the skies of Israel and Saudi Arabia, and then Patriot missiles soaring up to destroy them, brought home to Americans, for the first time perhaps, that America needs effective defenses against possible missile attacks," writes Heritage policy analyst Baker Spring. "No congressman or senator now can afford to be seen as opposed to missile defense....The SDI debate now shifts to what kind of defenses are best and when they will be built."

But precisely to avoid Congressional debate, the Heritage Foundation report calls on Bush to soon ask Congress for a "straight up-or-down vote" on the administration's proposed budget for a "stream-lined" SDI project called G-PALS, or Global Protection Against Limited Strikes. "This will press Congress to come out openly either in favor or against deployment of anti-missile defenses." The Heritage Foundation and other military industry-backed think tanks keep close tabs on Congressional members' voting records, and are liable to use the "soft-on-defense" line against incumbents in the 1992 election campaigns.

Not a Clear Shot

Even while the Heritage Foundation lobbies for more weapons expenditures, however, senior vice-president Burton

Yale Pines, writing in the Spring 1991 issue of the *National Interest*, calls for a renewed "conservative" foreign policy debate. He himself lands on the "America First" end of the spectrum. "For a conservative, the only legitimate goal of American foreign policy is the creation of a world environment in which America is left alone and at peace, in which America can trade and raise its living standards, in which Americans can expand their options and enrich their lives," Pines argues.

Underlying the differences between the Quagmirists and the Opportunists as to the net effects of the Gulf war, is a much larger post-Cold War debate about the role of the federal government—domestically, in the management of the economy and internationally, in terms of how much military and diplomatic intervention is necessary to insure U.S. competitiveness.

This debate on the Right has emerged through an ironic process. After decades of pouring national resources into an arms race and a fortress of executive-branch agencies to fight the "Communist Menace," the end result is a bureaucratized warfare state that is bankrupting society's infrastructure. Now right-wing activists are in a quandary. Some want to keep feeding the beast, for ideological and/or career opportunity reasons. Others have spent the past decade trying to reign in the welfare parts of the State through a variety of "deregulatory" processes, most notably by shifting the tax burden away from the rich. Some within this latter camp see the end of the Cold War as the all-clear sign for a new type of "containment"—against the bottomless pit of federal spending. They're after changing the kind of foreign interventionist policies that require a bloated military budget. But they're equally eager to do away with federal spending for things like public education, housing and environmental clean-up. Some within the pro-government spending faction—though committed to the sovereignty of corporations over average citizens—do think the State has a responsibility to insure (very) minimal standards of public welfare.

Above the fray stands the Bush administration which, unlike its predecessor, operates more like a junta than the elected expression of a political party or movement. Few "conservative" activists have access to administration decisionmaking, as they did under Reagan.

They're left to fight among themselves. In the March 1991 issue of the "Rothbard-Rockwell Report," put out by the Center for Libertarian Studies, Paul Gottfried blasted the big right-wing corporate foundations and think tanks, labeling them a bunch of pro-government "neoconservatives." In May Pat Buchanan, the standard bearer for the anti-neocon camp, parroted Gottfried's missive in his own syndicated column, and laid down the gauntlet between what he calls "traditional conservatives" and those pantywaist neocons. "Before true conservatives can ever take back the country, they are first going to have to take back their movement," fired Buchanan. Free Congress Foundation President Paul Weyrich—an "Old Right"-style ultra-Catholic who opposes libertarianism's loose morality and isolationism—jumped into the stew with his third position, "cultural conservatism." In a letter to the *Washington Times*, Weyrich accused Gottfried of sour grapes over his own rejection by neocon foundation grantmakers. Meanwhile, in July the neocon *American Spectator* featured a hit piece on Pat Buchanan, complete with a cartoon of an over-stuffed, leather clad Buchanan on a motorcycle, tossing a Coors beer can over his shoulder toward the prim, suited William F. Buckley and George Will.

From a tactical standpoint, the Right's current disunity affords progressive voices some ideological space. Many on the Right are now willing to say that U.S. foreign policy is, in fact, costly and chaotic. That recognition is a small chink in the administration's armor. If nothing else, it proves that the Vietnam Syndrome is still breathing.

But the Right won't do what the Left can do. The Right won't take principled stands against human rights abuses wherever they occur. The Right won't make the connections between "quagmirist" military adventures and the racial and economic injustices that underlie them. The Right won't call for the kind of necessary Pentagon cuts and budgetary redistribution that would alleviate the country's real economic and social problems. Ultimately, neither the Quagmirists nor the Opportunists will advocate a radical transformation of the corporate warfare state—because it's their lifeblood.

Free Market Environmentalism

Z Magazine, December 1991

Environmentalism poses a unique challenge to the usual guardians of the status quo. Were all things possible, corporate profiteers would just as soon enjoy clean air and water along with the rest of us. But there's one species of green stuff that takes precedent over all others. Environmentalists—especially those committed to a social justice approach—ought to expect opposition on a variety of fronts.

Thus far, corporate and government responses to "radical" environmentalism are taking shape in at least four forms: physical violence against activists and whistleblowers; covert and legal harassment of movement groups; the construction of an ongoing propaganda campaign against "ecoterrorists;" and, most subtly, the corporate-sponsored building of a "free market" answer to growing public concern about the environment.

Full coordination among the various players is not evident. Nor is it necessary to have a destructive effect. Those who write anti-Earth First! newspaper columns can, even inadvertently, create the kind of hostile political climate that gives a green light to physically violent conspirators.

Direct Action

The May 1990 car bomb assassination attempt on Earth First! leaders Judi Bari and Darryl Cherney remains unsolved. The whole set of circumstances surrounding the FBI and local law enforcement's mishandling of the case effectively sends a message that activists are fair game for anti-environmental vigilantes. In March 1991, Greenpeace scientist Pat Costner's rural Arkansas home and office were burned to the ground in what investigators consider a case of arson. The apparent target was Costner's 20-year collection of research material on toxic waste.

Writing in the July/August 1991 issue of the *Humanist* magazine, Political Research Associates analyst Chip Berlet chronicled stepped up police and legal harassment of environmentalists across the country. Activists have been jailed illegally without charges or bail. Local authorities, private spook agencies and even the EPA have begun collecting photographs and dossiers, as if to prepare for future covert operations against the movement.

The FBI itself spent $2 million to set-up Arizona Earth First!ers for an alleged conspiracy to sabotage nuclear facilities. Last summer's trial proceedings, in which the prosecution accepted defendants' plea bargain to lesser charges of vandalizing a ski resort, revealed just how far the feds are willing to go to bust up the movement. One of the government's informants within the Arizona group was a heavy LSD user named Ron Frazier who was subjected to FBI hypnosis sessions as part of his "training." The seedier sides of the Arizona case escaped much press scrutiny, in sharp contrast to the barrage of media speculation about whether Judi Bari, a single mother of two young daughters, might have blown herself up as a publicity stunt.

Seeing Red

The timing of one strident piece of anti-environmentalist disinformation was particularly striking. A week before scheduled Earth Day events in northern California, the San Francisco Sunday *Examiner*, on April 14, 1991, featured "Tale of a plot to rid Earth of humankind." It was a tale, alright. The story, by a Jonathan Tilove of Newhouse News Service, reported as credible the assertions of ex-CIA officer Vincent Cannistraro that a cabal of "radical environmentalists" were cooking up a recipe for a virus that could kill humans but leave other species unharmed. The *Examiner* featured the article on page 2, with a photo of Earth First! cofounder David Foreman.

Cannistraro concocted his mad-scientist fantasy while on staff with the National Strategy Information Center, a CIA-linked think tank that publishes books and holds conferences to promote "low intensity conflict" and "terrorism" as cornerstones of U.S. military doctrine. As a sidekick to Oliver North on the National Security Council, Cannistraro helped manage the CIA's funding of contra leader Arturo Cruz. NSIC president Frank Barnett is a veteran of the Cold War era Institute for American Strategy, itself a spin-off of the private American Security Council. Since 1955, the American Security Council has provided dues-paying corporations with intelligence reports on U.S. citizens, including the kind of information the FBI is prohibited from circulating.

Last May Cannistraro told Zack Stentz, an environmental reporter for the *Anderson Valley Advertiser*, that he's an "environmentalist," too and that he had no intention of defaming Earth First! "The environment just isn't something we focus on here," Cannistraro told Stentz. But disinformation and psychological warfare are things the NSIC focuses on, and propaganda might be most effective if it doesn't claim to be factual, but merely leaves readers feeling fear and loathing toward environmentalists.

Psy-war might also work best if its sources are multiple and difficult to track down. Newhouse reporter Jonathan Tilove also relied on an anonymous letter advocating biological warfare against humans, published in a 1984 Earth First! newsletter. Tilove lifted this tidbit from a 1990 report prepared by Cato Institute analyst Doug Bandow on assignment for the Heritage Foundation.

Bandow's paper "Ecoterrorism: the Dangerous Fringe of the Environmental Movement" was released as a Heritage Foundation "Backgrounder" in April 1990, marking the 20th anniversary of the first Earth Day. The purpose of these "Backgrounder" reports is to provide free ammunition to the Heritage Foundation's cultivated list of media hacks, coast to coast. Coinciding with heightened media attention to environmentalism, Bandow's paper rehearsed a litany of activist "crimes" against private property and portrayed "radical" environmentalists as spaced-out nature worshippers and misanthropes.

But Bandow also hinted at some of the essentials of an anti-environmental movement strategy. He reported that "the Washington Contract Loggers Association [has] created a Field Intelligence Report to track the activities of ecoteurs and has established a reward program for information leading to the apprehension of such criminals. Similarly, the Mountain States Legal Foundation, based in Denver, Colorado [has] established an ecotage hotline...In the first two months of hotline operation, Foundation President William Perry Pendley received reports of ecotage from California, Colorado, Idaho, Nevada, Oregon, and Washington. Mountain States [has] also established a clearing-house to file civil damage actions against saboteurs and to assist the government in prosecuting violators."

Aside from advocating increased intelligence gathering and collaboration between states and corporate-backed law firms, the point of Bandow's paper was to initiate a classic divide-and-conquer strategy, by positing "ecoterrorists" as a threat to "main-stream" environmentalists. "The best defense against ecotage is for mainstream environmentalist community and political leaders and for businessmen [sic] to speak out frequently on the issue," Bandow stressed. He explicitly slammed David Brower, veteran leader of the Sierra Club and Friends of the Earth, for having given office space to Earth First! and for defending its civil dis-obedience tactics. Bandow advocated that "mainstream" environ-mentalists purge the movement of radicals in the same way that "in the 1950s the American labor movement purged itself of most communist members and influence....The political organizations closest to the terrorist group's ideological views should separate themselves from its activities and help mold a broad social con-sensus against its activities."

Shoring Up Bulwarks

Shortly after the Heritage Foundation released Bandow's version of the divide-and-conquer proposal, another Heritage affiliate published an intelligence report on Greenpeace. The Capital Research Center tracks dissidents and provides its big cor-porate benefactors with early warning of anti-capitalist trends.

Here, too, the backgrounds of the Center's Executive Committee members are telling. Frank Barnett of the spooky National Strategy Information Center is on board. Richard Allen, head of the Heritage Foundation's Asian Studies Center, was Reagan's first National Security adviser, before he had to resign over the embarrassing revelation that he had accepted an expen-sive wristwatch from the Japanese government. Heritage trustee Midge Decter, who founded the recently disbanded Committee for the Free World, has taken credit for launching the National Association of Scholars and the whole hullabaloo over "political correctness." Norman Ture was a Reagan administration Treasury Department official and a key architect of tax cuts for the rich.

Capital Research Center's "Organization Trends" report expands the notion of "fringe" to include Greenpeace. The apparent rationale is the discovery that some activists have worked with both Greenpeace and Earth First!, and the fact that Greenpeace helped Earth First! hire a detective to solve the Judi Bari bombing case. Greenpeace is charged with "hostility to free enterprise" because it "condemns pirate whalers, specific toxic polluters and 'commercial greed.'"

But what really irks Capital Research Center is Greenpeace's organizational success: its millions of grassroots supporters and its near independence from corporate donations. Greenpeace has developed good relations with some of the "established" environmental groups, like Friends of the Earth and the Cousteau Society and, according to the Capital Research Center, "is drawing more 'mainstream' groups to the left." The Center recommends that businesses decline to donate to environmental groups. "Corporations might be tempted to shore up the 'moderates' as a bulwark against Greenpeace and organizations like it but the fact is that the entire movement is inherently anti-corporate."

Planting a Cash Crop

Some farsighted corporations are finding that the best "bulwark" against "anti-corporate" environmentalism is the creation and promotion of an alternative model called "free market environmentalism." Here the idea is not to pit "radical" environmentalism against a crude, devil-may-care capitalist message. The preferred plan is to cultivate a "reasonable" approach based on "balancing" the "individual rights" of big corporations with the rights of society and the planet to survive into the 21st century. "Free market environmentalism" has sprouted into a virtual cottage industry for a slew of libertarian-oriented think tanks, publishers and conference organizers.

At the vanguard is the Montana-based Political Economy

Research Center, started in 1980 by a group of Montana State University professors. Its advisory board includes an impressive list of academicians. Its board of trustees includes executives from the oil, chemical and financial industries. With generous funding from corporate foundations, including Carthage, Bradley, Earhart, Scaife, the Liberty Fund and the M.J. Murdock Charitable Trust, PERC sponsors educational seminars for undergraduate students and for journalists assigned to the environmental beat. PERC's photo-filled newsletter conveys the think tank's laid-back approach to political advocacy. These are the kind of people who wear fuzzy flannel shirts and Levi's and enjoy the great outdoors. But their love of nature is matched by their commitment to corporate sovereignty.

PERC's leading thinker is Montana State economics professor Terry Anderson. With coauthor and PERC associate Donald Leal, Anderson's book *Free Market Environmentalism* was published last spring by Westview Press, in a joint deal with the Pacific Research Institute in San Francisco. The "property rights paradigm" boils down to the argument that "market incentives" are the key to both protection and clean-up. Expansion of private ownership—including eventual control of what are currently public lands and resources—will increase environmental integrity. That's because "individuals," including corporations with the legal status of individuals, will want to protect the price or value of what belongs to them. Local community input on problems like toxic waste sites, deforestation or the construction of nuclear power plants is all well and good, but, lacking actual "ownership," the public has little incentive to make sound decisions. Should people living in an environmentally threatened area organize politically and pressure government agencies to restrain corporations on their behalf, this "command-and-control environmentalism" will threaten "democracy" because no one will be able to make an unlimited amount of money. The free marketeers invoke formerly "communist" governments' disastrous mishandling of environmental problems as if to prove that only individual property owners ought to make decisions for everyone concerned.

The elitism of "free market environmentalism" is only one of its many flaws. In a lengthy telephone interview, I queried

Professor Anderson about the obvious problems when a company like Exxon can accidentally destroy a huge part of Alaska. His quick answer was that high liabilities ought to be an integral part of what he calls "making incentives matter." In other words, if Exxon knew it would have to pay exorbitant penalties and litigation costs, it wouldn't hire drunken ship captains. But this argument, of course, assumes rationality and forethought on the part of corporate decisionmakers. It also neglects the fact that the only way to build into the "incentive structure" a liability high enough to restrain short-term greed is through political pressure, i.e., when citizens use "democracy" to force some sort of representative state agency to limit what cápitalists can get away with.

Recycling Free Market Advocacy

The "free market environmentalism" concept is fertilizing a number of corporate-backed think tanks. In general, the role of think tanks is to frame the terms of policy debates before they arise and to generate the kind of empirical data activists can use to influence policymakers. Since environmental problems are multifaceted, there's room for numerous organizations to develop expertise in special areas.

Citizens for the Environment, started in 1990 as a spin-off to the Washington, D.C.-based Citizens for a Sound Economy, has chosen to focus on solid waste management at the regional and local level. Because CSE has built a claimed membership of 250,000 since 1984 and functions as a lobby against taxes and government regulation of industry, its new advocacy on environmental issues is liable to fall on receptive ears. In a June 1991 conference on "The Politics and Science of Garbage" CFE drew speakers from the Environmental Protection Agency, from the plastics and packaging industries and from two "respectable" environmental groups, Resources for the Future and the Natural Resources Defense Council. Transcripts of the conference presentations indicate that a major theme was the need to privatize recycling, landfill use and hazardous waste management systems. In an interview, CFE director Stephen Gold expressed concern that local governments are "dictating to the private sector" because "the public's demanding a solution, like a lynch mob."

In June the libertarian Cato Institute launched its own Environmental Studies program with a two-day conference on "Global Environmental Crises: Science or Politics?" attended by about 200 people. Cato assembled an impressive array of scientific experts, including climatologists and meteorologists, with diverse viewpoints on the hot topic of "global warming." Cato's Environmental Director Robert J. Smith acknowledges that there's serious scientific debate on the extent of this crisis. But in a memo following the conference, Smith alluded to the Institute's political concern that "many government leaders continue to rush toward the June 1992 United Nations 'Earth Summit' in Brazil determined to bring central planning to all the world's nations on the basis of presuppositions about the world's climate." Environmental hazards caused disproportionately by First World polluters are not to be solved through multilateral diplomacy.

Both Citizens for the Environment and the Cato Institute receive major backing from Charles G. Koch, whose $15 billion a year oil and gas corporation is one of the largest privately held firms in the world. Koch Industries specializes in oil pipeline production but also has subsidiaries dealing with crude oil transport and coal mining. Koch has been the mainstay of the libertarian movement—which just happens to be the political tendency most actively pushing "free market environmentalism."

Acting Locally

In the next few years, much of the environmental debate is likely to occur on the state and local level. It's, therefore, no coincidence that in the past decade, the Right's biggest growth industry has been the formation of small public policy institutes, already numbering 55 in 29 states. A recent study by the National Committee for Responsive Philanthropy, a liberal group that monitors trends in the foundation world, reported on the Madison Group, which is coordinating activities among the new state institutes and some of the more established national advocacy groups. (The Madison Group is a project of the American Legislative Exchange Council, created in 1973 to organize right-wing state legislators.) Member think tanks in the Madison Group include the Political Economy Research Center in

Bozeman, Montana, and the Pacific Research Institute in San Francisco.

The Colorado-based Independence Institute, with a $200,000 budget and a donor list dominated by oil and coal companies, has begun issuing position papers on environmental questions most relevant to the southwest. Here, obviously, water is the central issue and the Independence Institute is applying "free market environmentalism" to advocate "water marketing." Proposals include conversion of state and federal water projects—already beholden to business interests—into totally private ownership. For starters, the Institute has recommended that Colorado "auction water rights to the highest bidders who meet reasonable standards," including the Audubon Society and the Nature Conservancy. But once water rights enter private hands, they're fair game for less conservation-conscious marketeers.

In the northwest, where clear-cutting and preservation of public lands top environmentalists' agenda, the counter-movement's catch phrases "wise use" and "multiple use" imply that forests can be exploited and preserved at the same time. Leading the charge for "wise use" is the Bellevue, Washington-based Center for the Defense of Free Enterprise. The group's v.p. Ron Arnold has been an active ally of Unification Church front groups, including the American Freedom Coalition which has promoted "wise use" in its monthly newspaper. Arnold makes frequent speeches for logging and oil industry associations. In 1990 Arnold told executives with the American Petroleum Institute that "they face complete destruction unless a serious public support movement is built at the grass roots non-profit level." Arnold's Center has also been raising funds for an apple growers' lawsuit against the Natural Resources Defense Council and CBS News over the defendants' claims that people were getting sick from eating apples sprayed with the chemical alar.

What Shade of Green?

Free market environmentalism threatens the genuine article not just because its proposals may give policymakers room to foot drag or pursue half-way measures, at the expense of the environment. The target audience for the free marketeers also seems to be the liberal and "moderate" activists who would just as soon not take on the root causes of environmental degradation. Though they can't be counted on to link true economic democracy with sane environmental policies, liberals do believe in citizen input on policy matters, and they have the kind of advocacy track records that make them the voices policymakers will listen to. Also, liberals sometimes condemn crude and violent attacks on dissidents. For these reasons and because they do reflect large constituencies, "mainstream" environmentalists can be tactical allies to social justice greens, on issues of shared concern. But coalition work between "mainstream" groups and those who see the connections of race and class to environmentalism will be threatened to the extent that free marketeers successfully frame policy debates in terms of property rights versus bureaucratic red tape. Given a respectable alternative that will ensure their access to economic and political elites, the liberal conservation-type groups just may jump on the "free market" bandwagon.

Blaming the Newcomers

Z Magazine, July/August 1992

If fantasy literature can provide clues about a movement's ideology and objectives, then one apocalyptic classic is especially ominous. Now circulating in English translation, *Camp of the Saints* grew out of the warped mind of French xenophobe Jean Raspali, in the wake of imperial France's defeat by Algerian nationalists. Raspali's psycho-novel has no actual plot or protagonists. It merely describes, in hyperbolic and occasionally pornographic prose, a nightmare scenario in which dark-skinned hordes from India's Ganges river area board the "Last Chance Armada" and make their way toward France's shores. Along the way, Raspali paints a picture of subhuman creatures who burn their own excrement as cooking fuel, fornicate with anything that moves on ship, and watch aimlessly while countless of their family members die like flies in the burning sun. All this is made possible by treasonous government officials and unscrupulous charities like the Red Cross, the World Council of Churches and the Vatican.

Camp of the Saints is sold through the classified ad section of *Spotlight*, the weekly newspaper of the pro-Nazi Liberty Lobby. Samuel Francis, a contributing editor of the "paleo-conservative" *Chronicles* magazine, referred to the book favorably in a syndicated column he wrote last January, in opposition to Haitian refugees' appeals for political asylum in the United States. The English-language edition of *Camp of the Saints* is printed and distributed by the American Immigration Control Foundation, one of the two largest anti-immigrant organizations in the country. AICF President John Vinson says he first read the book 16 years ago and that it profoundly changed his world view.

Sanctioning Xenophobia

Late last year California Governor Pete Wilson made headlines when he publicly blamed immigrants and poor people for the state's financial crisis. In a November 18, 1991, interview with *Time* magazine, Wilson answered questions about California's strained budget by naming "illegal workers" and "their children" as key culprits. For this and similar immigrant-blaming statements, Wilson took a fair amount of criticism, not only from human rights groups but also from liberal political opponents and from the *Los Angeles Times*. Wilson back-pedaled and refocused the blame on the federal government, which collects about two thirds of the taxes immigrant workers pay, but then doesn't redistribute that revenue to state-level social service agencies. By March Wilson publicly assailed presidential candidate Patrick Buchanan as a "racist," in an apparent effort to shore up his own image as a "moderate."

Meanwhile, the mainstream press presented dueling sets of statistics on the net societal impact of immigrant workers and their families. One study cited showed that the numbers of immigrant recipients of Aid to Families with Dependent Children was proportional to their numbers in the state's population. Analysts from two right-wing think tanks, the RAND Corporation and the Cato Institute, were quoted to the effect that immigrants not only pull their weight economically but that they subsidize the Social Security system and, especially in the case of undocumented workers, pay more into the system than they take out. Less altruistic than coldly calculating, some conservative economists favor increased rates of immigration as a means of keeping businesses "competitive." In other words, the more available workers, the lower the wages they'll accept.

Directly anti-immigrant arguments referred predictably to the issue of newcomers' school-aged children. Through no fault of their own, these kids burden a system unwilling to prioritize public education. This line of argument panders to the stereotype that people of color produce "too many" children. In reality, it is bigotry that has been breeding out of control for a long time.

Anti-immigrant sentiment is as old as the land grabbers who first followed Columbus. Governmental policies toward immigrants, and socio-cultural tolerance for these policies, have shifted with the economic winds. During the labor shortage of World War II, the United States welcomed Mexican migrant workers, and called them "braceros" (helping hands). But once the braceros were no longer needed, during the 1950s, the Immigration and Naturalization Service (INS) launched "Operation Wetback," and deported hundreds of thousands of Mexicanos and U.S.-born Mexican-American citizens.

It's not surprising that anti-immigrant violence has escalated in recent years, as part of a larger category of hate crimes. Fueling the economically-driven tension that causes increased hostility to immigrants are political leaders' endorsements of blame-the-victim ideology and, at the grassroots level, the circulation of racist propaganda like *Camp of the Saints*. The latter feeds the steady increase of organized hate groups. In February, the Klanwatch Project of the Southern Poverty Law Center in Alabama announced a 25 percent increase in the numbers of Ku Klux Klan, neo-Nazi and skinhead groups active from 1990 to 1991.

These groups attract the kind of individuals who've been victimizing people of color at increasing rates. In February the Federal Civil Rights Commission released a report documenting the relationship between politicians' Japan-bashing and increased harassment of Asian Americans. Also in February the American-Arab Anti-Discrimination Committee released its findings on hate crimes (assaults, bombings, arson, destruction of property) against Arab-Americans, up from 39 cases reported in 1990 to 119 in 1991. Not surprisingly, the increase correlated with the anti-Arab media campaign led by war-mongering elected officials. In late April of this year, a 19-year-old white San Diego man got in his car and chased five Mexican migrant workers through a border area neighborhood, fired a pistol several times and killed 23-year-old Humberto Reyes Miranda.

The lion's share of the violence against undocumented immigrants is perpetrated by U.S. police agencies. The American Friends Service Committee sponsors a Mexico-U.S. Border Program that compiles data gathered by dozens of human rights groups working together on the Immigration Law Enforcement Monitoring Project. The Project focuses on the five key areas of the country in which 70 percent of all Border Patrol detentions take place: San Diego, southern Arizona, El Paso, the Lower Rio Grande Valley and South Florida. In its latest report, "Sealing Our Borders: the Human Toll," as of February 1992, the AFSC reports ongoing patterns of "law enforcement" agency abuse against immigrants and also against U.S. citizens crossing the border. Of the 1,274 cases of abuse AFSC documented during a two-year period, about 28 percent involved verbal threats, insults and psychological harassment; about 22 percent involved physical abuse, including beatings, sexual assaults and shootings. Smaller numbers of cases included illegal searches, due process violations, and detentions of U.S. citizens. Between May 1989 and May 1991, AFSC reports seven cases in which Border Patrol agents killed Mexican citizens.

In the aftermath of the Los Angeles rebellion against police brutality and systemic deprivations, the Border Patrol was among the police agencies dispatched to arrest people. Los Angeles Police Chief Daryl Gates blamed the riots largely on Latino immigrants. The INS kicked into high gear with sweeps of workplaces and residential areas.

In a cheap bid for votes during a tough Congressional race, Orange County Rep. Dana Rohrabacher sent a telegram to President Bush demanding that the INS deport "illegal aliens"— and he didn't mean the extra-terrestrial kind. According to the *Los Angeles Times*, within the first week after the Rodney King verdict, about 1,000 of those arrested in connection with riots were "illegal" Latino immigrants; they were systematically turned over to the INS, to be deported.

Organizing Bigotry

Official acts of violence and disdain toward immigrants, "illegal" or otherwise, send a green light to the free-lance racists whose actions get too little attention. Several years ago, white supremacists organized a "Light Up the Border" campaign in which they repeatedly parked and directed their headlights toward Mexico, presumably, to make nighttime border crossings more intimidating than they already are. This spring, Tom Metzger of the San Diego-area White Aryan Resistance (WAR) announced an anti-immigrant demonstration at the border on June 7. One organizing leaflet for this "American Spring" action advertised: "Free soft drinks and hot dogs for all....four live bands to entertain you....Photograph thousands of future illegal aliens lining up on the border....They are coming by the millions and they are all pregnant!"

Among the numerous anti-immigrant activists in southern California, not all have connections to Klan-type groups, but some do. In a lengthy telephone interview from her home office in Long Beach, Ruth Coffey of Stop Immigration Now! kept reminding me in raspy tones: "I'm no skinhead. I'm 67 years old." Last fall Coffey addressed a meeting of the Los Angeles chapter of the Populist Party, an off-shoot of the pro-Nazi Liberty Lobby. The L.A. Populist Party is headed by neo-Nazi activist Joe Fields, who's running for a California State Assembly seat from the Long Beach-San Pedro area. (Fields has been a major subject of investigation by the progressive group People Against Racist Terror, which monitors neo-Nazi activity.) Coffey is an inveterate writer of anti-immigrant guest columns and letters-to-the-editor, which she manages to have published in newspapers across the country. Most of Coffey's verbal venom spews toward Mexicanos and Latinos. "Your country is on the verge of becoming a minority dictatorship," she warns.

Coffey is busy photocopying and circulating petitions urging members of Congress to support five anti-immigrant bills drafted by Rep. Elton Gallegly, a Republican from Ventura County's Simi Valley. The proposed bills include two that would require tamper-proof Social Security and identity cards for legal residents; one that would increase the number of Border Patrol agents; and one that would more severely punish drivers who transport undocumented immigrants across the border. The most politically dangerous of Gallegly's bills, however, is House Joint Resolution 357, a proposal to amend the Constitution so that U.S.-born children of "illegal" and "legal" immigrants are not "natural" citizens entitled to the same rights of other children born here. One of the southern California Congress members already on board this draconian bandwagon is Rep. Anthony Beilenson, a Democrat representing the Beverly Hills area.

Even if Gallegly's bill dies on the legislative vine, it's a useful anti-immigrant rallying theme for groups like the Stamp Out Crime Council (SOCC) in San Diego. The Council plays a limited lobbying role because of its "educational" tax-exempt status, but some of its members have recently formed a separate Coalition for Immigration Law Enforcement (C-FILE), which does lobby and endorse candidates. SOCC holds monthly dinner and lunch meetings with local politicians, sheriffs and police chiefs, and serves as a networking mechanism for cops and their friendly citizen-helpers who see crime everywhere. Mostly the Stamp Out Crime Council circulates literature on the supposedly related problems of "illegal aliens," drugs, pornography, welfare and declining educational standards. Barbara McCarthy, editor of the Stamp Out Crime Council's monthly "Eleven Ninety-Nine" newsletter (11-99 is a police radio code for emergencies), recently had one of her anti-"illegal alien" articles published in the "paleo-conservative" Rockford Institute's *Chronicles* magazine.

Though the anti-immigrant theme has been a mainstay of the Right's alternative press, the number of articles linking "illegal aliens" to welfare crises has increased slightly in recent months, and the attack has come from "paleo-conservative" allies of Patrick Buchanan. The weekly *Human Events*, which absorbed the mailing list of Buchanan's biweekly newsletter once he entered the primary elections, regularly attacks immigrant rights. One of Buchanan's advisors, Llewellyn Rockwell of the Ludwig von Mises Institute in Alabama, recently called for the restriction of immigrant citizenship rights in *Conservative Review*, Roger Pearson's latest publishing venture. (Pearson, who once headed the World Anti-Communist League, is a veteran white supremacist and long-time publisher of racialist and eugenicist "intellectual" journals.) Two staples of anti-immigrant literature are the obligatory photos of Mexican "illegal aliens" running perilously from INS agents across traffic on San Diego freeways, and the requisite folk lore about "legions" of pregnant Mexican women arriving in Texas just in time to suck up free childbirth services and "instant citizenship" for their newborns.

Two national organizations provide much of the "research" ammunition for the grassroots anti-immigrant groups. The American Immigration Control Foundation, based in Monterey, Virginia, includes among its board of advisors Jerry Woodruff, a Buchanan campaign consultant. AICF president John Vinson was an editorial writer for the Savannah (Georgia) *Morning News* before, he says, he read Jean Raspali's *Camp of the Saints* and became an anti-immigration activist. When I asked Vinson why he thinks immigration is such an important issue, his first response was that the United States faces the potential for regional or civil war, and—several days before Rodney King's police attackers were acquitted in Los Angeles—he predicted urban riots, driven by the "explosive mixture" of unskilled ethnic minorities. Vinson thinks the answer is to patrol the southern border with federal troops. But he thinks that won't happen because "there are powerful groups in this country that profit a great deal from out-of-control borders and massive immigration." The leading conspirators, according to Vinson, are the large corporations that want "free markets" and cheap labor. "The country is being flooded and even colonized by outsiders," says Vinson. AICF sustains itself by purchasing right-wing mailing lists and sending out about one million pieces of direct mail each year. Through direct mail, AICF has amassed 100,000 subscribers to its monthly "Border Watch" newsletter, which alerts readers to anti-immigrant legislation and gives contact information for local anti-immigrant groups.

More slick than AICF, but still transparent, is the Federation for American Immigration Reform (FAIR), a $2 million a year operation that emphasizes the "ecological" rather than "cultural" dangers of U.S. immigration policy. FAIR's national board of advisors includes a few "population control" liberals like former Senator Eugene McCarthy, Anne Ehrlich and Paul Ehrlich. FAIR takes money from the notorious Pioneer Fund, which sponsors "academic" studies of Black genetic inferiority. In a 1986 memo, John Tanton, founder of FAIR, U.S. English and several related groups, asked supporters rhetorically: "Will the present majority peaceably hand over its political power to a group that is simply more fertile?.... Can *homo contraceptivus* compete with *homo progenitiva* if borders aren't controlled?"

With headquarters in Washington, D.C., since 1979, FAIR only recently opened branch offices in Sacramento and San Diego. At the helm of the Sacramento office is Alan C. Nelson, the former INS Commissioner for the Reagan administration.

Timed to impact public debate shortly before California's June 1992 primary, on May 19 FAIR released to the press the results of a Roper poll it commissioned. FAIR spent $45,00 to conduct a detailed survey, with both national and California-specific samples. Questions were carefully worded so as to elicit high rates of responses to the effect that current immigration rates are too high and are impacting society negatively; that political leaders have been ineffective on the immigration issue; and that tougher laws against "illegal aliens" are in order.

Most questions produced anti-immigrant responses in the 70 to 90 percent range, lending the impression of a national consensus. In fact, in the current political climate, when people are asked questions like: "do you think the laws need revising," most may answer affirmatively without knowing anything about existing laws.

A bare majority of fifty-five percent polled positively toward the idea of a temporary moratorium on all immigration into the United States. FAIR is now calling for a three-year moratorium, and will use the poll results to lobby policymakers. "We would like to see politicians vying for people's votes take a position on this issue," said FAIR spokesperson Ira Mehlman at a San Francisco press conference announcing the poll results.

To maximize the media punch of the Roper poll, FAIR held simultaneous press conferences in Sacramento, San Francisco, Los Angeles, San Diego and Washington, D.C. In all of these cities, progressive civil rights groups found out about the FAIR poll ahead of time and were able to prepare their own press packets for interested reporters. At the San Francisco conference, for example, the Coalition for Immigrant and Refugee Rights and Services distributed background information about FAIR and factual refutations of common anti-immigrant myths. Also at the San Francisco press conference Ira Mehlman answered a question about FAIR's view that "illegal aliens" provoked the recent L.A. riots by claiming that a "wave" of increased immigration from Mexico has caused massive unemployment among African Americans.

Only by uniting the causes of immigrant rights, civil rights and organized labor can we combat this effort to blame one group's economic struggle for the plight of another.

Easy Racism

Nativist bigotry toward immigrants, especially those who can be defined as "illegal," is politically useful to the Right on two scores. First, anti-immigrant activism perpetuates the most retrograde aspects of our popular culture and, specifically, fuels the ranks of racialist and neo-Nazi hate groups. At a time when some traditional Klan-style recruiting tactics have become passé, the relative acceptability of anti-immigrant violence extends the life span of the white supremacist movement.

Secondly, elected officials who can't solve real social problems, but want to stay in office, can displace public discontent by picking on the most vulnerable members of, for example, the Chicano-Latino community. Civil rights organizations, then, must continue to protect people from the most brutal physical attacks and economic deprivations, instead of progressing toward the necessary goal: mobilizing disenfranchised peoples' voting potential. As the United States moves toward a North American "free trade" agreement that will allow money and jobs—but not human beings—to move "freely" across borders, elites would just as soon do without more pesky voters demanding things like better wages, environmental protections and respect for the sovereignty of all *Americans*.

Old Right Soldiers Never Die

Z Magazine, January 1994

There I was again, dressed up and ready to spend a day with people whose politics I deplore, this time at a modest Quality Inn hotel just south of San Francisco. What drove me across the Bay bridge before sunrise was the chance to observe first hand a group of self-described "paleoconservative" intellectual types in action over Halloween weekend. They gathered for the annual meeting of the John Randolph Club, a discussion group formed in 1990 on the eve of the Gulf War to forge unity among libertarians and conservatives who trace their political pedigrees back to the Old Right of the 1930s and 1940s. In those days, the Right fought bitterly against reformist New Deal benefits for the working poor and against the U.S. government's determination to enter the war against fascism.

John Randolph was a contemporary of Thomas Jefferson who had warned the "founding fathers" of the dangers of government expansion. The modern day "paleoconservatives," an odd mix of Christian Rightists and economic libertarians, are few in number and hostile toward what they disdainfully call the "official conservative movement." They use the "paleo" prefix, meaning "old," as a slap to their arch-nemeses, the "neo" conservatives, whom they hold chiefly responsible for the New Right's supposed sell-out to the welfare-warfare state.

For the uninitiated, some of these distinctions may obscure the Right's real fights over "free trade," U.S. militarism and the nature of the threat to "western civilization." I sat through the Randolph Club meeting because I wanted to hear how these right-wing intellectuals perceive their political opportunities. For the Right, as for any social movement across the spectrum, strategic success is tied, first, to activists' clear reading of their circumstances. Here I found right-wing thinkers who, if nothing else, understand their dire prospects but remain so committed to a purely anti-egalitarian philosophy that they will not say "die."

In the Center Ring

Three tiny think tanks employ the leading figures of the paleoconservative movement, such as it is. The Rockford Institute in Illinois publishes the slick and erudite monthly *Chronicles* magazine and a slew of research monographs on the supremacy of the nuclear family. From Auburn University in Alabama, the Ludwig von Mises Institute produces an equally impressive quantity of journals, newspaper and magazine articles, all from the perspective that the state has no business curbing the excesses of capitalism. The Center for Libertarian Studies in California keeps some of the same Old Right writers in print. Its new book *Reclaiming the American Right*, by Justin Raimundo, is a battle cry against the neoconservatives and their allies.

Added to the three think tanks are two nationally syndicated paleoconservative columnists. Samuel Francis regularly uses his *Washington Times* column to sound the alarm on illegal immigration. Joseph Sobran, another inveterate nativist, has, until recently, made his career as a protégé of *National Review* publisher William F. Buckley. For several years, Buckley has tried to stifle Sobran's frequent denunciations of Israel and the "Jewish lobby." Buckley recently fired Sobran after he wrote about a private conversation in which Buckley reportedly expressed an allegiance to Jewish neoconservatives and contempt for working class Catholics.

Sobran's dismissal was a hot topic at the weekend conference. The Buckley-Sobran feud had intensified during the months preceding the Gulf war when, along with Patrick Buchanan, Sobran had inflamed pro-Israel rightists with his anti-war rhetoric. As a group, the paleoconservatives opposed the Gulf War not only because they viewed it as a boon to Israel but also because they see no "national interests" at stake in post-Cold War conflicts. On this, the paleos were far outgunned by those on the Right who endorsed Operation Desert Storm. (Principals of the pro-war Coalition for America at Risk were later indicted as unregistered foreign agents of the Kuwaiti regime.)

In 1992, the paleos were among presidential candidate

Buchanan's most ardent supporters, and in 1993 the paleos were welcome speakers at two gatherings convened by Buchanan's new American Cause Foundation. Beyond that, though, the paleos typically find themselves preaching to their own small choir.

The John Randolph Club meeting, "The War on the Real America," drew only about 100 people, offered some predictable sessions and a few surprises. The first panel addressed what Joseph Sobran termed the "rhetoric of victimhood," which, he says, places all sorts of people in protected categories and then obliges the government to treat everyone as either victim or oppressor. Racism, anti-Semitism, sexism and homophobia, Sobran said, are terms that "all serve the same accusatory function," as the search for prejudicial motives "turns into a kind of gnostic crusade against an invisible, palpable evil." For Sobran, "homophobia" is the worst addition to the lexicon of victimhood. Homosexuality is not analogous to being black or Jewish, Sobran said, because—regarding Judaism—"however absurd you may think it is as a religion, it has held people together for thousands of years." No, homosexuality, Sobran said, is "a perennial disorder. It's something we don't want to happen. It's disabling."

Next, panelist Ron Paul, the libertarian former Congressmember from Texas, pontificated on some of the "real" victims of state authority. These include anyone who won't pay their taxes or obey "handicapped only" parking signs. Truck driver Reginald Denny is a "frustrating" case, Paul said. Denny's forgiveness toward the Los Angeles rioters who attacked him is all well and good, but now Denny wants a fat settlement from the city for its failure to provide adequate police protection. The function of government, Paul said, is to "guarantee our property and our rights to life and liberty, but not to meddle in social organizations and economic forms."

Fine. On this lofty philosophical plane, the paleoconservatives' concern with the proper role of the state is a discussion any progressive might find provocative, if not convincing.

The second panel, though, plunged straight into the gutter. Justin Raimundo, an openly gay man, warmed up the audience with his argument that the Right should oppose civil rights laws both for gays and for racial minorities. The trouble started when conservatives lost the battle over the 1964 Civil Rights Act. "Today property rights have been upstaged by civil rights," Raimundo said. The only way to challenge the "whole paradigm" of gay rights is to "challenge the egalitarian premises of the civil rights movement." (I later asked Raimundo to elaborate, and he told me he, frankly, doesn't care if someone wants to discriminate against him because he's gay.)

Next to speak was Jared Taylor whose book *Paved With Good Intentions* blames continuing racial strife on liberal policies like affirmative action. Taylor let loose with one of the wildest racist diatribes I can ever recall hearing. "Blacks as a group," Taylor said, "in all of recorded history have never done anything to suggest that they as a group are equally intelligent as all other races in the world."

I looked around. No one flinched. Taylor proceeded to cite chapter and verse from various studies "proving" genetic IQ differences between the races. He concluded that it is a "disservice to tell blacks and Hispanics that they're just as good" as whites and Asians because part of growing up is realizing that there are people superior to oneself.

Taylor won enthusiastic applause. He was followed by Michael Levin, a philosophy professor from the City College of New York. Levin is notorious for pushing racist and sexist theories. In his Randolph Club speech, Levin claimed that "men on average are a little more intelligent than women." He blamed crazy ideas about gender equality on the "absurd belief," legitimized by the Supreme Court's 1954 ruling against segregated schools, that there are no differences between the races. In order to be consistent, the general public accepted egalitarian women's movement propaganda, just as they had earlier "conceded" to arguments against racial discrimination.

I looked around again. Still, no one batted an eyelash. I wondered: was this San Francisco, 1993? Or had some time machine carried us all back to Mississippi 30 years ago?

Only Justin Raimundo openly disputed Jared Taylor's and Michael Levin's biological determinism. From the floor, two of the other paleos, Thomas Fleming and Samuel Francis, gently challenged Taylor's linkage of the term "success" to the notion of racial IQ differences. One can be a happy brick layer, Francis noted, without scoring high on intelligence tests.

The Red Carpet

I quickly ducked out of the hotel to find some fresh air and a private lunch down the street. I later asked people casually what they thought of the morning panel on genetic racial and gender IQ differences. Staffers from the Center for Libertarian Studies did not endorse the panelists' biological determinism. But they claimed the audience was receptive because the whole topic is "taboo." Where else can one hear it openly proposed that poverty is rooted in our genes? (Yes, and where else but at a KKK rally can one burn a cross and call it "free speech?")

I chatted with an elderly physician who had travelled all the way from Minnesota. He agreed with Jared Taylor that black people are just plain dumber, and he suggested I read Carleton Putnam's *Race and Reason*. I reminded him that this was a tract distributed by the segregationist white Citizens' Councils back in the early 1960s. He just smiled.

Never before had I attended a right-wing conference with such friendly folk. This was a novel experience. The conference organizers, from the Center for Libertarian Studies and the Ludwig von Mises Institute, know my political orientation. Some read *Z Magazine*. Yet my hosts treated me in a truly hospitable, even collegial, manner. I was graciously introduced to some of the very same characters whose politics I have routinely scored in print. These are big boys who don't take themselves so seriously that they can't jostle with the enemy.

After lunch, Joseph Sobran caught me buying a pamphlet at the literature table. "Don't you have enough damaging material on us yet?" he joked. "No," I said. "I can never get enough. I'm a bottomless pit."

It was a surreal moment, one that said something about the possibility that people who hate each other's politics might still treat each other with respect. Our opponents are not monsters to be feared but, rather, regular guys and gals whose regressive ideas we can only defeat through education and organization.

On the Edge

The paleoconservatives can afford to be charitable toward someone like me because—for all their prolific publishing—they are thoroughly marginalized even from fellow rightists. The late afternoon conference panel was billed as a strategy session with the paleos' heavy-hitters: columnist Samuel Francis, libertarian economist Murray Rothbard, Rockford Institute President Allan Carlson, and Dr. Gary North, a leading Christian Right advocate of "dominion theology."

Francis had nothing to propose except that paleos stop thinking their job is to *prevent* a revolution and instead realize that it is time to overthrow the existing regime. "We should be essentially counter-revolutionaries," Francis said. Murray Rothbard, who twenty years ago was known as the "godfather" of the libertarian movement, likewise had nothing to recommend. He spent his time denouncing "big government libertarians" who, in their quest for power, had allied themselves with elites in favor of NAFTA and egalitarian school "choice" initiatives.

Rockford Institute president Alan Carlson had a plan. Since home-based economies are largely exempt from government interference, the answer is to make the family a "self-recreating counterweight to the state." Start a vegetable garden, raise a flock of chickens, educate your children in home schools. "Forego USDA choice steak and eat yogurt from your own goat," Carlson quipped. "Build new institutions and let a thousand flowers bloom." Gary North urged a high-tech solution. The advent of cheap CD-ROM computer discs makes it now possible to pack hundreds of volumes of classic Old Right texts into user-friendly study kits for Christian home schools. "The microcomputer, my friends, is the Saturday night special of communications," North said. But other paleos were not convinced. Some argued that the only way to get a good education is to go to a library and read real books.

No one seemed to want to argue about what it might take to build a real, influential political movement. Sectarians of all stripes would rather fight than cultivate allies. Samuel Francis captures the plight of his Old Right comrades in the title of his new book, *Beautiful Losers*.

From the 1940s forward, U.S. right-wing movements have engaged in varying degrees of conflict, compromise and collaboration with one regime after the next. A half-century struggle against "communism" united libertarians and moral traditionalists with ideologically dominant Cold War liberals. The Buckleyites and later the New Right-Christian Right leadership had the foresight to make themselves indispensable to the Republican Party and its corporate benefactors. In the process, the Right's "new majority" faction dropped crude biological racism and made common cause with pro-Zionist neoconservatives, many of whom are Jews. Now, absent the facade of anticommunist unity, the Old Right's "paleo" heirs—with their core tenets of nativism, "free market" economics, and military noninterventionism—find themselves alienated even from the conservative movement they helped build.

Around the time of the Gulf War, some few on the left were beguiled by the anti-war rightists who seemed to share their anti-statist, anti-Zionist views. The most vocal of the anti-war rightists were the same paleoconservative figures now agitating against immigrants, queers and assorted egalitarians. No one should have thought for one moment that the Right's post-Cold War military jitters had anything to do with justice. Some unlikely political alliances are both necessary and based on principle. Others are simply beyond the pale.

Part III
The Patriot Movement

The U.S. Taxpayers Party

The Guardian, October 9, 1991

George Bush's New World Order is so unpopular among many right-wing activists that they're quietly setting up an "anti-establishment" Taxpayers Party in time for the 1992 presidential race. But unlike some of the third party projects initiated by splinter groups in the past, this latest effort represents a coalition of forces beginning to work together for the first time.

The U.S. Taxpayers Alliance is the brainchild of New Right strategist Howard Phillips who has already recruited Taxpayers Party coordinators in 25 states. Phillips, who founded the Conservative Caucus and helped start the Moral Majority, says his current goal is to qualify Taxpayers parties for ballot status in most states by 1992. The party plans to run a presidential candidate who can attract disaffected voters to a platform that includes opposition to taxes, welfare, foreign intervention, legal abortion, federally funded education, and affirmative action. The USTA favors deployment of SDI, expanded use of the death penalty, and deregulation of industry.

Phillips says his top choice to head the Taxpayers presidential ticket is "Crossfire" talk show host Patrick Buchanan. In a survey Phillips sent to USTA supporters in June, 40.7 percent said they wanted Buchanan to run for president; another 22.5 percent favored Jesse Helms, and 13.4 percent favored Oliver North. Phillips is working behind the scenes to persuade Buchanan to run, but declines to say who his second choice would be.

With a budget this first year of only $140,000—and no donation larger than a thousand dollars—Phillips says he has no illusions that the U.S. Taxpayers Party will win more than a tiny percentage of the vote in 1992. "I'm sacrificing the present for the sake of the future," Phillips said in an interview, explaining that the USTA doesn't expect to see real results for eight to twelve years. But Phillips contrasts his current game plan with threats he made, during the late 1970s and 1980s, to lead a factional revolt from the Republican Party. This time, he says, activists outside the Republican mainstream are more likely to join him because they have no strong, unifying figure like Ronald Reagan to keep them hitched to the GOP.

This latest in a series of right-wing third party efforts differs from its predecessors in at least two other respects. This one is not intended as a symbolic move aimed at winning short-term concessions from the Republican Party platform committee, nor is the goal to influence candidate selection, even on a local level. Also unlike some of the earlier third party efforts of the past two decades, when sectarian factions emerged under the banners of the Libertarian, American Independent and Populist parties, this new coalition represents a more deeply-rooted merger of tendencies within the Right.

In his monthly letter to supporters, Phillips profiles the state coordinators who've agreed to start Taxpayers parties in their particular states. What's clear is that the USTA is uniting factions without prior histories of collaboration but which have a potential to attract large numbers of already organized people. From the ranks of the John Birch Society—which, contrary to popular perception, still has thousands of hard-core members—Phillips has recruited *None Dare Call it Treason* author John Stormer to head the Missouri party and pro-South Africa activist Donald McAlvany to head the Colorado branch. Ed McAteer, who helped Phillips start the Moral Majority in 1979, will lead the Tennessee party. From the militant "Reconstructionist" wing of the Christian Right, Rev. Joseph Morecraft of Georgia and George Grant of Florida will head their states' parties. From the racist Right, Phillips has recruited a former George Wallace campaign organizer to run the party in North Carolina and a former anti-busing activist to do the same in Delaware.

On board the USTA's platform committee is Lewellyn Rockwell, who heads a libertarian think tank in Alabama and who has spent the past several years helping to build a so-called "paleo-conservative" alliance of right-wing Christian libertarians. In various states, USTA is regrouping the remains of earlier splinter parties, such as the Independent Voters party in Massachusetts and the American Independent Party in California.

USTA's recruitment from the racist right has aroused the ire of its major competitor. The neo-nazi Liberty Lobby has recently launched a Populist Action Committee, which plans to back state and local candidates across party lines, but with special attention toward Populist Party presidential contender Lt. Col. James "Bo" Gritz. In July, Liberty Lobby's weekly *Spotlight* newspaper published a hit piece on Howard Phillips, chastising him for being insufficiently anti-Israel and for not backing segregationist Alabama governor George Wallace in his 1968 presidential campaign.

Phillips is likely to be perceived as poaching on some of Liberty Lobby's turf. Both the PAC and the USTA pitch to right-wing circles angered at the Bush administration's unwillingness to slash taxes and gut civil rights more severely. Both groups' constituencies opposed the Gulf War and distrust administration overtures toward the Soviet Union and East European countries. But over the years Phillips has been involved in fewer factional squabbles than the Liberty Lobby and, though Phillips is willing to work with racists, his Taxpayers Party message centers around economic issues. "All of the problems that concern me will be solved if we get rid of the income tax," Phillips said. The Liberty Lobby also opposes taxes but racism and anti-Semitism have been its raison d'être.

The 24-member board of Liberty Lobby's Populist Action Committee includes "former" Mississippi Ku Klux Klan leader Robert Weems and former White Citizens Council organizer John Rarick. Liberty Lobby recently sent its supporters a fundraising letter for the planned gubernatorial race of "former" Klan leader David Duke, now a Louisiana state Senator.

Phillips doesn't carry this kind of baggage. But he does have a proven track record for what he calls "organizing discontent." He resigned as head of the Nixon administration's Office of Economic Opportunity in 1974 and went on to form the Conservative Caucus and other organizations credited with Ronald Reagan's 1980 victory. Since then, Phillips says, he has continued to push for a third party. In 1988 he backed the Libertarian Party's presidential candidate, former Texas Congressmember Ron Paul.

Phillips' professed opposition to foreign aid and government intervention in the economy has to be considered in light of his years of ardent support for "constructive engagement" with apartheid South Africa, one of the most striking cases of state control over "free" markets and labor. More than any single activist on the Right, Phillips has lobbied vigorously for U.S. aid to Jonas Savimbi's UNITA operation in Angola. Like other right-wing libertarians, Phillips opposed the Gulf war because, he says, it was not "to protect proximate vital interests" and because the U.S. fought under the flag of the United Nations.

As the various taxpayers parties gather steam, they're liable to play the somewhat positive role of chipping away at President Bush's aura of popularity while raising public consideration of third party possibilities. Despite the unlikelihood of a presidential win, the taxpayers parties—and the grassroots machinery they might energize—can make inroads on issues decided at the state and local levels.

Howard Phillips correctly sees third party building as a long-term proposition, and he's banking on the kind of economic downturns that will give his message greater resonance. "My hope is that there will be circumstances in which people are so upset at the way things are going that without even necessarily knowing or buying into all of the things that we advocate or believe, they will support us in protest against the things they disapprove," Phillips said in an audio tape circulated to USTA supporters. "The medicine we're prescribing doesn't taste good and people are only going to take it when they have no choice."

'Populists' Tap Resentment of the Elite

The Guardian, July 3, 1991

Add this to your list of grotesque political alliances to be concerned about: the Liberty Lobby, representing the largest collection of racist and anti-Jewish leaders in the country, has just formed a new "Populist Action Committee" to help elect candidates and to forge a multi-organizational movement based on anti-elite resentment.

In recent weeks, the Liberty Lobby's weekly *Spotlight* newspaper has featured a series of articles on the new PAC, described as "non-partisan, devoted to the principles of populism, nationalism and the U.S. Constitution, for America first." The initial line-up of advisory board members includes a former Ku Klux Klan leader, a former Air Force intelligence officer and a number of veterans from Liberty Lobby's 1984 and 1988 Populist Party campaigns.

With subscriptions totalling in excess of 100,000, the *Spotlight* is the largest-circulation publication on the Right.

Though the acronym is PAC, the new Populist Action Committee is not intended to be a political action committee (PAC) for legal purposes. The Federal Election Commission (FEC) defines a PAC as an organization that finances electoral campaigns, and requires PACs to report their expenditures. Liberty Lobby's PAC brochure says it will "promote and publicize populist candidates, urging patriots around the country to make direct contributions to these candidates." PAC will thus avoid having to report its activities to the FEC, and it will be able to wield influence with selected candidates from the two major parties as well as with those running as Libertarians or "independents."

The new Populist Action Committee is the latest in a long chain of efforts by "anti-establishment" rightwingers to unite around opposition to U.S. military intervention abroad and, at home, against government measures to alleviate poverty and institutional racism.

The racist Right surged in the wake of the Supreme Court's 1954 decision mandating public school integration. As the civil rights movement grew, so did the scores of white citizens councils, spurred on by the 1957-1958 creation of Liberty Lobby by veteran racist organizer Willis Carto. In the late 1960s, Liberty Lobby rallied around the presidential candidacy of segregationist Alabama Governor George Wallace.

It was Carto who created the infamous Institute for Historical Review, to promote pseudo-intellectual "theories," such as the one that the Nazi holocaust is a figment of Jewish propagandists' imaginations. By the 1980s, Carto created an electoral front called the Populist Party, around which Liberty Lobby would coalesce a movement beyond the pale of Ronald Reagan and George Bush. In 1988, "former" Klan leader David Duke ran for President on the Populist Party ticket. The visibility he gained then enabled him to win a seat in the Louisiana state legislature in 1989.

The newly formed Populist Action Committee has announced an initial advisory board of 24 far-right leaders. These include: former Mississippi Ku Klux Klan leader Robert Weems; former Louisiana Congressmember and white Citizens Council organizer John Rarick; Tom Valentine, host of *Spotlight's* "Radio Free America" talk show, broadcast weeknights over the Sun Radio Network; Retired Army Lt. Col. James "Bo" Gritz; and Retired Air Force intelligence officer Col. L. Fletcher Prouty.

Prouty is well-known among anti-CIA researchers and activists across the political spectrum because his 1973 book *The Secret Team* was one of the earliest exposés of CIA misdeeds. What's less known about Prouty is that for several years he has been a cause célèbre of Liberty Lobby, appearing frequently as a guest on Tom Valentine's "Radio Free America." At Liberty Lobby's September 1990 annual convention, Prouty told the crowd that "if anybody really wants to know what's going on in the world today, he [sic] should be reading the *Spotlight*."

Those who do read the *Spotlight* are treated to a regular fare of "news" reports and features aimed at the tastes of racist and anti-Jewish "populists." Numerous ads for mail-order literature and upcoming events promote "Christian Identity," a mix of white supremacy theory and a distorted reading of the Old Testament. Scores of little non-denominational Identity churches around the country preach that Jews are the "seed of Satan" and that non-Aryan ethnic groups are subhuman "mud people."

In international affairs, *Spotlight* frequently covers South Africa from the point of view of the pro-apartheid Conservative Party, now at odds with the reformist de Klerk administration. *Spotlight* regularly lauds French fascist leader Jean Marie Le Pen and his National Front. At a May 21 meeting to announce the new Populist Action Committee, Liberty Lobby's special guest speaker was British nazi leader John Tyndall, Chair of the British National Party.

Liberty Lobby vigorously opposed the U.S. war in the Persian Gulf, in large part because of the war's ostensible boost to Israeli interests. Beyond this kind of isolationism—which is traditional among home-grown fascists—Liberty Lobby's recently printed list of agenda items includes opposition to: "so-called civil rights laws," "tax-supported housing" and "use of tax funds for abortion." Liberty Lobby says it's all for, among other things, "outlawing the Communist Party" and the "right of states to establish voter qualifications," the latter being a prescription for the old property ownership restrictions that kept black people disenfranchised throughout the South.

In recent years, *Spotlight* has reported frequently on some of the same issues that concern the Left: U.S. intelligence ties with drug traffickers, martial law continency plans proposed by the Federal Emergency Management Agency, and the fact that Israel absorbs a huge portion of the U.S. foreign aid budget. Currently, *Spotlight* is heavily focused on the "October Surprise" evidence that the 1980 Reagan-Bush campaign arranged for the Iranians to withhold release of 52 U.S. hostages in exchange for favorable weapons deals beginning in 1981.

The problem is that Liberty Lobby and other self-professed "anti-establishment" rightists frame these stories not within the context of the real political-economic system in which they occur, but rather as the work of "secret teams" or cabals of bankers and

Jews.

Particularly in hard times, people who are hurting are vulnerable to the idea that their economic problems stem from a secret conspiracy rather than from capitalism's organized crime.

Assuming that the racist Right's agenda reaches farther than the handful of candidates it may support in 1992, and assuming that the economy is liable to get worse before it gets better, the new Populist Action Committee has an ominous potential. It can appeal to the interests of many working and middle class people, who can't identify with the corporate and political elites who run this country, but who can be encouraged to look for "the enemy" among the Jewish-sounding surnames on the *New York Times'* masthead, and among the non-white bodies lined up outside soup kitchens and the local unemployment office.

Patriots on Parade

Z Magazine, September 1992

While most people spent the Fourth of July picnicking or relaxing, I spent the holiday weekend cooped up in Sacramento's Hyatt Hotel with 300 Christian patriots. For two days, leading lights of the patriot movement shared some of their planned revenge tactics against the Banking Conspiracy operating out of the Federal Reserve Board. They met under the banner of the National Coalition to Reform Money and Taxes, founded by twenty patriot groups at a similar conference in Denver, Colorado, a year ago. This coalition does not include respectable New Right tax reform groups like the National Taxpayers Union or the Howard Jarvis Taxpayers' Association in California. The coalition does include plenty of Identity Christians who preach a racist and anti-Jewish dogma, and holdovers from the now-defunct Posse Comitatus, a largely rural network of white supremacists who organized among bankrupt farmers during the 1980s. The conference was not about how to get a rich corporate class to pay its fair share of taxes, nor was the agenda about directing tax revenues away from the Pentagon and toward a social infrastructure. No, these patriots don't want any of their hard-earned money going to build schools and hospitals. Let the ungodly fend for themselves.

The crowd at this patriot conference was a sight to behold. Slightly less than half were women, and most of them were as unadorned as I was. (If only I, too, had dishwater blonde hair and a turned-up nose, I would have felt perfectly at ease in my standard denim skirt and flat shoes.) Men's hairstyles ranged from crew cuts to pony tails, and three kinds of get-ups seemed most in vogue: ill-fitting blue suits, mechanic-style coveralls, jeans and T-shirts. From the podium, one speaker joked about how hard it was to keep his own pants up. But physical appearance mattered not to those assembled for the greater goal of, as one patriot put it, "making the IRS' lives a living hell." One of the patriots was a black man, and one of the leading speakers was jury trial expert

Godfrey Lehman, who is ethnically Jewish and lives in the San Francisco Bay area.

What distinguished this patriot conference from the dozens of right-wing gatherings I've attended over the years was a palpable sense of paranoia among participants. Tickets for the two days sold for twenty-five "federal reserve notes" (cash) or an equivalent blank postal money order. That was so there'd be no trace of a transaction for the IRS to follow. There was no conference registration list, no "Hello, my name is" lapel stickers. Even the people staffing the literature tables were tight-lipped toward curious strangers. The patriots must have assumed the hotel was swarming with undercover IRS agents. As indicated by the on-stage speakers—all of whom did wear name tags—the object of the tax protest game is to jam the government bureaucracy with an unending series of lawsuits and declarations of non-citizenship, all of which must be financed through off-the-books business schemes of questionable legality. The patriots' personal outlaw behavior dovetails with their do-or-die worldview.

"There are some people who think the current fiat money system has no alternative but to collapse, and it could be in the near future," proclaimed Coalition Chair Brett Brough at the start of the two-day event. "I feel excited about that. But what is important is, somebody has to pick up the pieces. Who is that going to be? Are you prepared to seize the day? It's going to end up being our job." The patriots never explained exactly how they intend to seize the day. Instead they spent most of the conference time introducing themselves and promoting their own pet projects and literature for sale. There was Richard Flowers of Oregon's Christian Patriots Association with a collection of books from John Birch Society and Aryan Nations authors. Gerard Beeman of the State Citizenship Service Center in southern California was on hand to teach patriots how to get rid of their Social Security numbers and stop being "voluntary slaves" to the Sixteenth Amendment. Bob Chamberlain of San Diego promoted a Missouri-based School for the Last Days correspondence course and a suspicious "alternative health insurance" program: you give them your cash and if you get sick, they send you to a network of doctors who've dropped their American Medical Association licenses. Paul Hall represented *Jubilee*, a virulently racist and anti-

Jewish tabloid published by Identity Christians in Mariposa, California. John Voss of Colorado directs the National Commodity and Barter Association, a network of "warehouse banks" for patriots who store their wealth in the form of precious metals.

After the opening prayer and introductions, the patriots reassembled across the street from the Hyatt, in the park behind the Capitol building, for a Declaration of Independence ceremony. At a precise moment, synchronized with patriots on the east coast, the tax protesters took turns solemnly banging on a liberty bell under the orange trees.

Back at the conference, the speeches were boring, but the literature tables were something else. What a rare opportunity to add some truly hard to find titles to one's collection of filth. One table stacked with Identity Christian tracts featured the *Jubilee* newspaper. In its current issue, *Jubilee* directed its readers to the 1938 classic, *Jewish Ritual Murder* and reproduced one of that book's woodcut drawings of Jews slitting a Polish girl's throat. In the same issue, an Identity preacher advocated stoning unbelievers to death. At the other end of the ball room, "Sovereign Advisor" publisher Gerard Beeman pushed a bound collection of articles about George Bush, photocopy-reduced from Lyndon LaRouche's *New Federalist*. Around the corner was the Christian Patriots' Association's spread of books, pale in comparison to some of the 1,100 titles listed in the free catalog: *Race Intelligence and Education, The Turner Diaries, Aliens and the American Tragedy*, ad nauseam. I bought a copy of Des Griffin's *Anti-Semitism and the Babylonian Connection*, and learned that Aryans have replaced their term for the United States, "Zionist Occupational Government" or ZOG, with a new one: "Babylonian Occupational Government" or BOG.

The Star of the show was Lt. Col. James "Bo" Gritz, the presidential candidate of the Populist Party. Gritz is a highly decorated Vietnam War hero (or criminal?) who has led several unsuccessful search-and-rescue missions for GIs still supposedly missing in action in Southeast Asia. Gritz' exploits, reportedly financed on one occasion by Ross Perot, inspired Rambo and other popular war revenge movies. In 1988 Gritz served briefly as vice-presidential running mate for David Duke's Populist Party presidential campaign. In 1991 Gritz joined the Liberty Lobby's Populist Action Committee, which has endorsed racist candidates running for local offices in many states.

I shook hands with "Rambo" and asked him why his campaign has received so little attention from the Liberty Lobby's weekly *Spotlight* newspaper. Gritz said he had refused to allow Liberty Lobby and Populist Party founder Willis Carto to run the campaign, so the *Spotlight* had turned on him. "The Lord is guiding this campaign," he shrugged. Anyway, hard-core tax protesters don't make their locations known by registering to vote, but those not on the lam had several choices this election year. Concurrent with the feud between Carto and Populist Party leader Don Wassall, Gritz' campaign was upstaged by the primary candidacies of David Duke and Patrick Buchanan.

In his Fourth of July speech, Gritz told the crowd: "It's time to have a soldier to lead." He then gave the patriots his battle plan: use the president's constitutional power to abolish the income tax and the Federal Reserve Board, strengthen the U.S. military, and get out of the United Nations. But just in case the patriots can't "take Capitol Hill," they'd better start "filling sandbags," and "be prepared to live in spite of the government." Gun control, he quipped, is the "ability to hit what you aim at with the first shot." To great applause, Gritz told one crude joke after the next. He said he looked forward to a day when the patriots would bury politicians' heads in concrete and "use what's left as bike racks."

Identity Christianity and the Posse Comitatus

Bo Gritz' campaign and the formation of the National Coalition to Reform Money and Taxes are only the latest episodes in the history of the Christian patriot movement. This movement differs from others on the Right in several respects. Its organizations are highly decentralized and transient and, more than anything that could be described as mainstream, the patriot movement is deeply rooted in an anti-establishment subculture that rejects consensus reality. Typically patriots dabble in unconventional health treatments and conspiracy theories about "secret team" assassinations, "suppressed technology," and even government collusion with visitors from outer space. To evade taxes, a lot of patriots run their own small businesses or live self-sufficiently in hinterlands where they can keep a low profile.

The two cornerstones of Christian patriot belief are Identity Christianity and opposition to the "debt money system." Organizationally, Identity churches and Posse Comitatus tax protest groups grew up together in the past two decades. Identity Christianity is an arcane racist gospel that now attracts much of the white supremacist movement. According to Identity doctrine, the Lost Tribes of Israel migrated, in Biblical times, from the mediterranean to the British Isles and Scandinavia. Their descendants settled in northern Europe and, later, in North America. God's true Identity or Chosen People, therefore, are not the Jews (who are Satan's offspring) but rather the Aryan nations of northern Europe. People of color are considered a separate subhuman species, and "race-mixing" is forbidden.

Earlier, in the 1940s, Identity was popularized by two racist preachers, Wesley Swift and Bertram Comparet. Swift was a Klansman who founded the Church of Jesus Christ, Christian in 1946. One of Swift's earliest followers was William Potter Gale, who recruited a following from his ranch in Mariposa, California. Another of Swift's disciples, Richard Butler, started the Aryan Nations compound in Hayden Lake, Idaho.

I pored through a microfilmed set of Gale's *Identity* newsletters to distill his teachings on the Posse Comitatus. In a constitutional republic, the theory goes, the county is the true seat of government, and the sheriff is the reigning law enforcement officer. The Posse includes all able-bodied adult men whom the sheriff can summon to preserve order and arrest government officials guilty of constitutional violations. According to Posse credo, the Congress has unconstitutionally expanded its power by taking away states' rights to make currency (gold and silver coins), by instituting a federal income tax, and by establishing a private Federal Reserve Board which manipulates interest rates to the advantage of the Jewish bankers who control it. In *Identity*, Gale also claimed that UFOs had been prophesied in the Old Testament Book of Ezekiel.

Wacko, yes. But thousands of "patriots" in hundreds of churches believe this stuff. The movement's lack of formal hierarchy allows each preacher to pick and choose which tenets and tactics to emphasize. Richard Butler has pastored the most violent Aryan Nations adherents. Robert Miles, an aging Klansman living in rural Michigan, blends elements of Norse paganism with Identity, and has organized Aryan cadre inside prisons. More than a dozen Christian radio stations broadcast the racist and homophobic rantings of Colorado's Pastor Pete Peters.

Several trends have fostered the spread of Identity Christianity in the past decade and a half. By the mid-1970s, following the gains of the civil rights era, Ku Klux Klan membership was down to slightly more than 1,000, an all time low. Identity became a useful pseudo-religious explanation for "who was behind" developments like "forced integration," the Middle East oil crisis and the inflationary economy of the 1970s. Identity also provided a racist alternative to the increasing popularity of evangelical Christianity, with its focus on Israel as the site of Christ's expected return. In the late 1970s, evangelical Christians mobilized within the Republican Party. Some white supremacists supported Reagan, but most were thoroughly alienated from electoral politics.

The farm crisis of the early 1980s provided an ideal recruitment opportunity for the Posse Comitatus wing of the patriot movement. There were plenty of progressive farm advocates. But the Posse built strongholds throughout the midwest (and southwest) with its demagogic conspiracy theories. North Dakota Posse tax protester Gordon Kahl became the movement's first martyr in 1983. After four months as a fugitive wanted for killing a federal marshal, Kahl died in a blaze of glory during a shootout with ZOG agents at an Arkansas Posse safe house. Kahl's death was followed by a series of crimes by the Aryan Nations' terrorist Order. In 1984 they killed Denver radio talk show host Alan Berg. Next, the Order pulled off a series of bank and armored car robberies; one Brinks heist alone netted more than $3 million. The federal government responded with force and indicted several dozen Aryan Nations leaders. A handful of white supremacists were convicted and jailed, but the movement survived.

Then and now, violent racists are a persistent threat to their immediate targets, but they hold little chance of winning political power. Their cyclic growth spurts and declines are a barometer signalling just how sick U.S. society can get. Despite a limited government crackdown, the movement maintains an estimated following of tens of thousands of "patriots."

Insuring the movement's survival has been a kinder, gentler periphery surrounding the terrorist hard core. Prior to the outbreak of racist violence in the 1980s, some patriots formed tax protest groups that could attract people not already immersed in the Posse Comitatus. In 1979 California tax protesters started the Constitutional Patriots Association, later renamed the Free Enterprise Society. No doubt many recruits have been unsuspecting victims of IRS red tape. The Free Enterprise Society has managed to get its tax protesters on KPFA-Pacifica Radio around April 15—without telling listeners the group's agenda and affiliations. (One FES activist was a staff engineer at KPFA for many years, before leaving the payroll a few months ago.) Even within the above-ground tax protest groups lurked Aryan Nations affiliates. One northern California Free Enterprise Society organizer was David Moran, a self-described "survivalist" and Identity disciple of William Potter Gale. Moran declared war on the "Zionist Occupational Government" and died in a December 1986 shootout with California highway patrol officers on the north coast.

Free Leona Helmsley!

Speakers at the Fourth of July National Coalition to Reform Money and Taxes (NCRMNT) shindig never managed to get down to brass tacks about how they intend to achieve their twin goals of eliminating taxes and the Federal Reserve Board. Vern Holland of the Freeman Education Association in Oklahoma fired off some new tactics on the tax protest front. He urged patriots to start suing individuals who purchase homes and other property seized from tax evaders: Tie so many of these people up in court that the IRS won't find any buyers for its ill-gotten gains. In the meantime, Holland and others have made contact with attorneys for Leona Helmsley, the jailed New York hotel operator and tax cheat. Holland said his plan is to latch onto the "Free Leona Helmsley" appeals case as a means to catch the media spotlight.

Sunday morning the Coalition was supposed to present reports from its working committee on tax and monetary reform. That never happened because the patriots couldn't stop promoting their pet theories. Vern Holland went head-to-head with fellow patriot Byron Dale over the gold standard. Dale was a South Dakota farmer (and colleague of Posse leader Gordon Kahl) who wound up losing his profitable cattle ranch when he insisted on paying off his loans with hay and wheat instead of cash. Neither Holland nor Dale could properly conjugate the English language, but they spent about an hour debating the necessity of gold and silver money. Dale argued against an immediate return to hard currency, on the grounds that most gold and silver is in the hands of "the bankers" anyway. Holland said he didn't care if all the banks in the United States collapsed tomorrow. Unable to make headway with Holland, Dale finally broke down, yelling into the microphone: "We've got to do something!"

Then I knew without a shadow of a doubt: for ten years I've been looking for the "lunatic fringe," and I finally found it.

Shifting the Blame

Z Magazine, July/August 1995

If there was any silver lining to the Oklahoma City bombing, it was the opportunity the incident afforded for public education and dialogue about the growth of right-wing organizations. A number of corporate press outlets made honest attempts to quickly come up to speed on the subject of the paramilitary militia movement. But there was also no shortage of the usual political grandstanding about "terrorism" coming from both the Left and the Right.

There was a rush to psychoanalyze militia members by attributing their fascination with guns and ammo to the rise of hate radio. Surely such media discourages rational debate between political adversaries. But high blood pressure radio may be as much a symptom as a cause of rising political violence. When a caller finishes ranting and raving over the airwaves, he— and it is mostly men—is just as politically disenfranchised as he was the night before. Hate radio arouses listeners' emotions but it gives even those on the far Right no real means to effect political change.

The political system is increasingly closed to all but the wealthy elite. Unable and unwilling to adopt the Christian Right's skillful use of mostly civil tactics like voting, lobbying, and public protest, the patriot movement is now armed and trigger happy. We can speculate about numbers—estimates range in the tens of thousands. This home-grown scare is not the work of just a handful of kooks. It comes out of a failed and reactionary system that has crushed progressive alternatives.

But even this kind of analysis can scarcely be uttered in respectable media environments. So corporate press hounds need to invent other explanations. One, based on the drive to lump all rightwingers together, is the claim that Pat Robertson, author of a nutty bestselling book *The New World Order*, instigated the Oklahoma City bombing by fomenting the latest round of popular conspiracy thinking.

Robertson's book, published in 1991, sold a half million copies in the aftermath of the Persian Gulf war. But *The New World Order* has attracted press attention only recently, now that Robertson's Christian Coalition threatens the Republican-Democratic party status quo. The book itself is a hodge-podge of popular conspiracy theory and pseudo-historical analysis. Chapter 1, however, raises the legitimate question of why the U.S. government looked the other way when Saddam Hussein's military prepared to cross the Iraqi border into Kuwait in the summer of 1990. From there, though, Robertson descends into some of the conspiracist Right's standard claims about how the United Nations is a threat to U.S. sovereignty; about how U.S. elites aided and abetted Communist regimes; about how elites also have encouraged the growth of an anti-Christian New Age movement.

Both the *New York Times* and the *New York Review of Books* have blasted Robertson for his chapter on "international" and "European" bankers. Such terms are well understood as code for the old canards about how Jewish bankers run the world. In his Bibliography, Robertson cites two notorious anti-Jewish writers, Eustace Mullins and Nesta Webster. He also cites reliable works: Marxist historian Larry Shoup's book on the Council on Foreign Relations and *Z* writer Holly Sklar's book on the Trilateral Commission. Contrary to press attempts to paint Robertson as a closet Nazi who relies on anti-Jewish sources, Robertson's citations are all over the map ideologically.

Nowhere does Robertson recommend that his readers break the law or try to overthrow the government. He ends *The New World Order* with a call for readers to join his Christian Coalition's work to contact registered voters in every precinct, city and state. As of 1991, Robertson's goal was "to see a pro-freedom majority in the United States Senate in 1992, and a reversal of leadership in the House of Representatives by 1996." Since 1991, Robertson has achieved his goals, and more. In 1994 the Christian Coalition spent one million dollars lobbying with mainstream Republicans to defeat Clinton's health care reform plan. In 1995, the Coalition spent another million dollars lobbying on behalf of the Republicans' Contract With America. This obeisance to the GOP has made the Christian Coalition anathema to many of the gun enthusiasts, tax evaders, white supremacists and paranoid John Birchers who have formed militias precisely because they fear and reject alliances with elites.

Now that the Christian Coalition, and the larger Christian Right movement it represents, has won a voice within the Republican Party, some political elites and media pundits are beside themselves with fear. Elites paid no attention to Robertson's nutty conspiracy theories back in 1991 when *The New World Order* climbed onto the *New York Times* bestsellers list. Back then Robertson was a useful Republican ally. Along with *New York Times* editorialists, Robertson supported the Persian Gulf massacre. In 1992 Robertson endorsed the reelection campaign of George Bush, against challenger Patrick Buchanan.

Since 1992, though, elites of both parties have been trying to contain the influence of the Christian Right. Rather than attack the movement for its reactionary policy goals—many of which are shared by leaders of both parties—the strategy of the Democratic Party and its press symps has been to try to portray the Christian Right as a "radical" movement at the fringes, not the center, of the political establishment.

The Oklahoma City bombing provided a perfect frame for media elites eager to smear the electorally-active Christian Right by putative association with "extremist" groups and actions. In a series of *New York Times* columns this year, editorialist Frank Rich has made a fetish out of Robertson's conspiracy book. Since the Oklahoma City bombing, Rich has tried to link Robertson and his 1991 book to bombing suspect Timothy McVeigh. In an April column, "New World Terror," Rich claimed that Robertson's politics are "identical" to those of Mark Koernke, the Michigan short-wave radio broadcaster whose sign-off slogan "Death to the new world order" made him a hit with militia men nationwide. In another column, "Connect the Dots," Rich summarized reports circulated by Planned Parenthood, which uses a broad brush to try to link a small number of violent anti-abortionists to a vast and conspiratorial paramilitary underground. Last year, Planned Parenthood publicized the fact that one violent anti-abortionist, Matthew Trewhella of Missionaries to the Preborn in Milwaukee, also advocates the formation of militias. Frank Rich uses this fact to promote the view of Planned

Parenthood researchers: by "connecting the dots," between right-ists who attend similar meetings and circulate similar propagan-da, one can incriminate a wide array of anti-abortionists as some-how connected to a network of neo-Nazis and even the Oklahoma City bombers.

The guilt-by-association rhetoric now used to identify mem-bers of what Rich calls a "national paramilitary subculture" sounds familiar. It is reminiscent of the charges, in the 1970s, that the anti-war movement was responsible for the violent acts of the Weather underground. Then, as now, such charges are at best intellectually dishonest and, at worst, designed to distract atten-tion from some inconvenient political realities.

Don't expect the *New York Times* to make a federal case out of Pat Robertson's political (and, in some cases, monetary) sup-port for the Nicaraguan Contras, the death squad governments of El Salvador and Guatemala and the murderous proxy armies for South Africa's apartheid regime during the 1980s. Don't expect any series of editorials about how Robertson used his "700 Club" program, in 1993, to jam the Congressional switchboard with constituent phone calls against the lifting of the ban on gays in the military. Killing and depriving people of their civil rights are not as newsworthy as the possibility that Pat Robertson may be a closet anti-Semite.

The media's recent focus on Robertson as conspiracist comes about a year into a rhetorical campaign led by the Democrats and some former allies of the Christian Right. In the spring and sum-mer of 1994, opinion polls showed that Republican Congressional candidates were headed for a landslide. Right-wing radio hosts and video producers were then dogging the Clinton presidency with endless scandal hype about Whitewater and Gennifer Flowers. In June of 1994, the Clinton camp fought back. Democratic Congressional leader Vic Fazio and Surgeon General Joycelyn Elders staged big media events at which they denounced the Christian Right, though not on any substantive grounds. Clinton himself went on a radio talk show and blasted Rush Limbaugh and Jerry Falwell by name.

The same month, coincidentally or not, the Anti-Defamation League released—for the first time ever—a book attacking the

Christian Right. Fresh from the public relations debacle over the 1993 press revelations that this "civil rights" group had been spying on leftists and Arab-Americans, the ADL compiled facts from previously published books and articles and wove them together in its characteristic guilt-by-association style. Secular and neoconservative Jewish supporters of the Christian Right went ballistic and charged the ADL with partisan politicking.

But central among ADL's themes—and the one that seems to have stuck in the craw of pundits like Frank Rich—was the charge that the Christian Right is particularly menacing to Jews. On the "700 Club," Robertson lamented the rupture of his long-standing friendship with ADL director Abraham Foxman, and denied the charge of anti-Semitism by flaunting his loyalty to Israel (as if the two were related.) More than any other religious broadcaster, for years Robertson has used his Christian Broadcasting Network, in the U.S. and in the Middle East, to broadcast "news" favorable to the Israeli government. ADL and other pro-Zionist groups have long relied on support from those evangelical Christians who read U.S. military aid to Israel as a Biblical mandate. But during the 1980s, the Christian Right-conservative Jewish alliance was sealed as much by anticommunism as it was by Zionism.

While researching my new book *Roads to Dominion*, I came across a set of documents at the Hoover Institution from the Reagan administration's Outreach Working Group on Central America. On a regular basis, more than fifty groups met secretly with White House personnel to coordinate media and lobbying activities on behalf of the Nicaraguan Contras. The Working Group included: Jerry Falwell's Moral Majority, Pat Robertson's Freedom Council, Maranatha Campus Ministries, the Heritage Foundation, Conservative Caucus, Accuracy in Media, Young Americans for Freedom; the neoconservative Institute on Religion and Democracy, the Ethics and Public Policy Center, the Jewish Institute for National Security Affairs and the Anti-Defamation League of B'nai B'rith. The meetings were conducted by officials from the National Security Council, the CIA, the Defense and State Departments.

In a real conspiracy, the Christian Right, the ADL, the New

Right and the neoconservatives worked together with U.S. intelligence agencies to promote murder and mayhem in Central America. Most of the same players rallied together again when the agenda was to bomb Iraq back to the Stone Age.

Then Robertson was just a quirky televangelist, and the Christian Right was no threat to the republic. Now everything has changed. The 1992 Republican National Convention sent a shock wave through much of the political establishment. Democrats and so-called centrist Republicans finally realized that the Christian Right is the single most influential faction within the GOP. Now that the movement has grown into something that cannot be stopped, politicians fear the Christian Right's grassroots clout on domestic policy issues. But the Democrats, the media pundits, ADL and its ilk will not publicly challenge the Christian Right for its promotion of mainstream policy goals: defeating health care reform, gutting welfare, tightening the "criminal justice" system. Instead, the attack of the liberals is narrowly confined to issues such as school prayer, around which the Christian Right can be made to appear truly "extreme."

There are links between the militias and some members of the Christian Right. And the militias pose an outright physical danger to whomever they happen to target. Liberals pundits and politicos want to throw a spotlight on loony rightwingers training in the woods for Armageddon. That avoids the question of how and why the majority of Christian Right activists are, step-by-step, using legitimate tactics to implement regressive policies.

If one opposes the Christian Right, does it matter if the attack on them is accurate and principled or merely expedient? It does not matter to unscrupulous liberals whose goals are to get Clinton reelected and to preserve this system of political and economic inequality. It should matter very much to progressives who want to make real change and who first need a clear picture of the opposition.

Patriot Games

The Progressive, September 1995

It was business as usual at the Fourth of July weekend Freedom Rally of patriot movement groups from northern and southern California. About 200 mostly middle-aged men and married couples spent two days at San Jose's Hyatt Hotel—swapping IRS war stories, alternative health tips, and some of the most virulent racist and anti-Semitic literature I've seen in more than a decade of monitoring the Right.

Three years ago, I attended a nearly identical gathering sponsored by the same group, and there were a lot of familiar faces. The Free Enterprise Society, founded in 1979 to provide unofficial legal advice to tax dodgers of the far Right, provides an annual forum for a loose network of racist preachers, conspiracy mongers and militia men. They came from up and down the state and from as far away as Colorado, Montana, Oklahoma and Missouri. There was one African American in the crowd and at least one other Jew besides myself. My WASPish, bearded, ponytailed partner was among about a dozen long-haired guys. The patriots dressed in a mix of cheap suits, shorts and T-shirts. The shirts on one pair of burly patriots had a modified Budweiser logo advertising Jesus Christ as the King of Kings. Other shirts read: "Fight Crime—Shoot Back," "Forget the Alamo—Remember Waco," and "Will Work for Freedom." The women, few in number, were nondescript. One wore her American flag lapel pin upside down.

The price, per couple at the door, was 45 "federal reserve notes" or f.r.n.'s. The patriots hate the U.S. paper money system, but until we return to gold and silver, they will accept the green stuff. Cash only, no questions asked, no name tags except for those worn by speakers and exhibitors. Unlike the Christian Right gatherings I frequently attend, the patriot events are not places where one easily strikes up conversations with strangers. Scribbling too many notes, too fast, on a legal pad, I drew some uncomfortable glances from the tight-lipped and paranoid.

Two months after the Oklahoma City bombing threw a spotlight on the armed wing of the patriot movement, the incident has not thinned the Patriots' ranks or toned down their rhetoric. If anything, these folks have added the arrest of Timothy McVeigh to their store of beefs against the government. Speakers and leafleteers were united in their claim that the feds bombed their own building to justify a crack-down on patriots.

The mainstream media and the general public have only recently discovered the militia movement. But among those assembled at the Freedom Rally were people who have spent more than fifteen years organizing within earlier streams of the far Right, particularly the violent Posse Comitatus tax resisters and the white supremacist Identity churches. These two overlapping networks grew out of the failed segregationist movement of the 1950s and 1960s. After the racist Right's heyday during the 1968 George Wallace presidential campaign, the movement foundered and split into innumerable sects. It never regained its massive influence at the ballot box. A remnant of the segregationist movement degenerated into small groups of gun-toting survivalists, including those who waged terror campaigns under the banner of the Aryan Nations in the 1980s.

Old patriots do not die. They just change uniforms. Small groups with names like the Free Enterprise Society, the Freemen Educational Association, The National Commodity and Barter Association, the Second Amendment Committee, the American Pistol and Rifle Association and, literally, hundreds of others, have been around for years, tilling and fertilizing the soil out of which the armed militias have recently sprung. Observers of the Right are currently debating the extent to which the new militia groups are dominated by old-fashioned Klansmen and Jew haters. We have a long way to go to arrive at accurate data on the numbers of active militia members, let alone a full picture of their beliefs and motivations. It is clear, though, that the militias are like fish swimming in a big blue patriot movement sea.

The Freedom Rally opened with everyone singing "The Star Spangled Banner." Montana tax resister Red Beckman then read every single word of the Declaration of Independence. John Voss reported the latest in the saga of the National Commodity and

Barter Association which was founded in 1979 by a Posse Comitatus leader. The goal was a network of interest-free banks through which Patriots could store their assets in the form of gold and silver coins. The IRS sees the NCBA as an illegal scheme by which Patriots hide their assets from tax collectors.

Next up was Eugene Schroeder, introduced as a founder of the American Agriculture Movement. Actually, the AAM was a farmer's organization that was infiltrated and taken over by Schroeder and other Posse Comitatus supporters in the early 1980s. Posse leaders were then trying to recruit and train displaced farmers for armed confrontations with federal agents. All over the Midwest, the Posse tried to convince troubled farmers that Jewish bankers, not a recessionary economy, were responsible for farm foreclosures.

From the Hyatt podium, Schroeder sang a different tune. He said nothing about Jews or farmers. He now lectures on how, beginning during the Depression, the Roosevelt administration invoked emergency constitutional powers to set up a secret government dictatorship.

The most popular speaker was Pastor Everett Sileven from the Faith Baptist Church in Houston, Missouri. Years ago, while pastoring in Nebraska, Sileven became a patriot movement folk hero when he went to jail rather than submit his church elementary school to state certification. Sileven came to San Jose to speak about the need for churches to become "unregistered" and truly free by rescinding their 501 (c) (3) tax status.

Sileven's literature table was stocked with tapes and pamphlets on the evils of "race-mixing." I bought a pamphlet that opened with the heading: "The Sin for Which God Will Kill: Inter-Racial Fornication by Copulation and Reproduction."

At the lunch break I chatted with the pastor about the theology he calls "Christian Israelism." Sileven acknowledged that he is an Identity Christian but he says he avoids the term "Identity" because it has become a derogatory "government and media" label. He explained to me that the ten lost tribes of Israel, described in the Old Testament, migrated and became the Anglo-Saxon people. That does not mean that all Anglo-Saxons are saved. But he said that "in the Kingdom"—code for the theocracy his brand of Christians plans to establish one day—only people of the white race will hold leadership positions. He assured me that other races won't be killed but will be allowed to live "in the Kingdom," if they obey "the Law."

In his talk on "unregistered churches," Sileven made references to his Christian Israelism. He also denounced churches that won't preach against the "wickedness" of: "the American monetary system, the income tax, race-mixing and multiculturalism, government schools, sodomy, women's lib and the United Nations." The Patriots shouted Amens and Hallelujahs and gave the pastor a standing ovation.

Next came five-minute pitches from each of the exhibitors. The most bizarre was Godfrey Lehman, a regular in California tax protester circles. Lehman is an elderly Jewish man from San Francisco. His mission in life is to reform the jury system, and to do so he networks with the Free Enterprise Society. Lehman used his time on stage to announce an upcoming meeting for a new militia group in—of all places—Berkeley, California.

At this and other patriot meetings, there was a gap between the content of formal, on-the-record presentations and the materials spread out on the literature tables. There was literature on how to "protect one's assets" by setting up off-shore trusts. There was information on how to file a form with one's county recorder's office declaring oneself to be a "state citizen" and, therefore, exempt from federal taxes. At one table a woman sold high-priced bottles of an "instant energy" liquid containing caffeine, along with Militia of Montana literature packets. There were guerrilla warfare training manuals and a directory of 1,800 patriot movement organizations.

There was also a large quantity of racist and anti-Semitic literature. Floyd Wright, an accountant and real estate broker from Grass Valley, California, pushed *The Controversy of Zion*, a thick volume on how Jews have controlled "government, large industries, banks, the media, etc." since the days of the Pharisees.

At another table, patriots lined up by the dozens to buy back issues of *Jubilee*, a twenty-four-page bimonthly tabloid which touts itself as "America's most popular Christian patriot publication." (In one past issue of *Jubilee*, an Identity preacher advocated stoning unbelievers to death.) Recent issues of *Jubilee* have reported on militia meetings and the latest theories about an "ADL/Reno Witch Hunt" to frame patriots for the Oklahoma City bombing. The paper is riddled with references to the "Jewish-controlled media" and swipes at "Kosher-conservative talk show host Rush Limbaugh." Items advertised include a "Hitler on Tape" series—English translations set with Third Reich music so you can "hear the truth for yourself."

Two tables down, there was an outfit called Dynamics of Human Behavior. Here exhibitor Madelyn Burley-Allen shared her table with Richard Charles, who ran as a write-in candidate for Congress from the Bay area last year, and whose business card had a Klan logo on it. From Burley-Allen I bought the latest issue of the *Christian Defense League Report* and read a long diatribe about how "Jews now have special rights in the United States that others do not have."

She gave me a free copy of the Sons of Liberty fifty-page book list. Most of the books were about Jews but there was also a short section on Race and Civilization. Titles included *Proof of Negro Inferiority* which, the catalogue said, distinguishes "differences in brain size between the races, compares white and non-white skeletons and compares Negroes to gorillas."

Copies of the *CDL Report* and this book catalogue were stacked on the table. But I watched Burley-Allen play a cute game of hide-and-seek with part of her merchandise. She kept a notebook over the word "Jew" on the cover of *The Biological Jew* by Eustace Mullins. This is a classic tract comparing Jews to parasites. Only when I asked to read something else on the table was she obliged to move the notebook and reveal the pamphlet's full title. It was like some sort of pornography shop where the vendor keeps the truly vile stuff behind the counter for special customers.

From the podium the Freedom Rally organizers urged everyone to shop at the tables. The overt display of hate literature raises the question of whether everyone in the patriot movement agrees with the racist and anti-Semitic themes. There is no way to know for sure. But no one at the rally raised an eyebrow about the hatemongering exhibitors, nor about the Posse Comitatus veterans who spoke. There is anecdotal evidence that this is standard fare at militia movement gatherings, and it's no surprise. The far Right political culture is steeped in hatred of designated enemies. It does not matter if all the patriots are racists. Their intolerance for agencies of the federal government seems to be matched by their tolerance for neo-Nazis in the patriot coalition. This coziness with virulent racism and anti-Semitism is not something to be taken lightly.

That's why I disagree with some progressives who see the anti-government militias as allies, or at least recruiting grounds, of the left. The argument is that the far Right includes many who, though misguided in some of their targets, at least understand that the real enemy is the capitalist state.

This argument might have some merits were it not based on false assumptions. The most obvious fallacy is the monolithic notion of "the people" versus "the government." Anyone who thinks that "the masses" are uniformly noble, or that they always act in the interest of fellow citizens, has only to study Germany in the 1930s and Chile in the 1970s. Our own history includes plenty of cases when white, working-class Klansmen terrorized African Americans as well as progressive white workers. And they did so not just because they saw racist and anti-labor activity as pertinent to their own narrow self-interests.

When progressives hear some of our own best pundits say that the patriots are our allies because they, too, are anti-government, we have to ask what it means to be anti-government. We oppose the ways in which agencies of the state serve to maintain wealth and power concentrated in the hands of the few, with deadly results for the majority. We oppose a corporate-controlled electoral system that effectively disenfranchises most people in this country.

The patriot response, over many decades and not just since Oklahoma City, has not been to try to figure out how we can all work together to redistribute wealth and power equitably. Their conspiracy theories are not just a temporary diversion; they are a reactionary substitute for accurate and principled analysis of the relationships between government and economic elites.

On the issue of taxes, the contrast between the far Right and the Left is revealing. Progressives oppose the government's failure to tax corporations for their fair share, but progressives believe that the costs of collective goods—roads, hospitals, schools, etc.—ought to be shared. In ten years of monitoring right-wing tax protest groups, I have never heard them discuss the disproportionate tax burden shouldered by the poor. Nor is opposition to corporate tax evasion part of the patriots' repertoire. The patriots want to avoid paying for services they routinely use, like everyone else, while they cast the income tax as part of a plot by Jewish bankers to control world finance.

Right-wing conspiracy theory is antithetical to the Left's opposition to entrenched power. Progressives oppose bad policies and out-of-control agencies. Right-wing patriots target entire races of people and small cliques of purported evil doers.

To position oneself as an ally of the militias is to give credence to the dangerous ideas of the broader patriot movement. Their ideas are not just loony but scary; they are loaded and aimed at real people.

Are the patriots more dangerous now than they were before? Yes and no. The numbers at the Freedom Rally were no greater than they were three years ago. Most of the speakers and organizers have been around for years. Most of these people have dropped out of electoral politics or vote for tiny parties such as the American Independent Party and the U.S. Taxpayers Party. But then, those who spent a full weekend and plenty of cash to attend the Freedom Rally represent the hard core, those already so convinced that they bat not one eyelash at the neo-Nazis in their midst.

What ought to worry us now are reports that the militia groups are drawing thousands of newcomers. Surely some of the new recruits are people who, in another era, might have joined a progressive party or social movement. The weakness of the organized Left has, by default, created greater recruitment opportunities for the conspiracist Right. People look for answers to their problems and fears, and a bad explanation is better than none.

The rise of these private armies—if we are to believe the estimates of tens of thousands of militia members—signals an unprecedented expansion of the patriot movement. Growth emboldens such a movement to move from rhetoric to dangerous action. Dangerous to the trigger happy militias' many potential targets, not just government agencies but to environmentalists, civil rights activists, women's health care workers, and anyone else who happens to be in the wrong place at the wrong time.

The most striking thing about the Fourth of July Freedom Rally was what went unsaid. No one was willing to examine even the unintended consequences of arming and training, en masse, for violent confrontations. No one was willing to take responsibility for the loose cannons among the ranks. Only a few short months after the atrocity of Oklahoma City, the patriots would not even pause to consider the deadly possibilities of marching toward doomsday.

Index

About the Author

Sara Diamond is one of the country's foremost authorities on the Christian Right and the other right-wing movements. She has conducted first-hand research on the U.S. Right since the early 1980s.

She holds a doctorate in sociology from the University of California at Berkeley and has taught journalism and sociology at several California universities.

She is the author of *Spiritual Warfare: the Politics of the Christian Right*, (South End Press, 1989), and *Roads to Dominion: Right-Wing Movements and Political Power in the United States*, (The Guilford Press, 1995).